The Well of the Saints

IRISH DRAMATIC TEXTS

THE WELL OF THE SAINTS

By J.M. Synge

Edited
with an Introduction and Notes
by
Nicholas Grene

The Catholic University of America Press
Washington, D.C.

Colin Smythe
Gerrards Cross, Bucks.

Library of Congress Cataloging in Publication Data

Synge, J.M. (John Millington), 1871–1909.
    The well of the saints.

    (Irish dramatic texts)
    Bibliography: p.
    I. Grene, Nicholas. II. Title.
III. Series.

PR5532.W4	1982	822'.912	82-4367
ISBN 0-8132-0571-9			AACR2
ISBN 0-8132-0570-0 (pbk.)			

British Library Cataloguing in Publication Data

Synge, J.M.
    The well of the saints.—(Irish dramatic texts)
    I. Title   II. Grene, Nicholas
    III. Series
    822'.8   PR5535.Y/

    ISBN 0-86140-127-1
    ISBN 0-86140-128-X Pbk

CONTENTS

ACKNOWLEDGEMENTS

Grateful acknowledgements are due to the Trustees of the Synge Estate for permission to make use of manuscript material in the preparation of this edition, to the Library of Trinity College, Dublin, and the National Library of Ireland for making such manuscripts available, and to the National Library also for permission to quote from the Joseph Holloway journals.

CHRONOLOGY

1871   John Millington Synge (pronounced sing) born 16 April in Rathfarnham near Dublin, youngest of five children of John Hatch Synge and Kathleen Synge, née Traill.

1872   John Hatch Synge dies.

1888   Enters Trinity College Dublin, where he studies Irish among other subjects.

1889   Enrolls at Royal Irish Academy of Music.

1892   Graduates from Trinity College Dublin.

1893   Goes to Germany to study music.

1895   First visit to Paris; between 1895 and 1903, spends each summer in Ireland and at least a part of each winter in Paris.

1896   Visit to Italy.

Meets W.B. Yeats in Paris.

1897   Briefly a member of Maud Gonne's Paris-based nationalist Irish League.

First operation on swollen glands on his neck, later diagnosed as Hodgkin's disease, lymphatic sarcoma.

1898   First visit to Aran, May-June; from 1898 to 1902 visits the Aran islands every year.

1899   Visit to Brittany.

1902   Writes *Riders to the Sea*, *The Shadow of the Glen* and the first draft of *The Tinker's Wedding*.

1903   Visit to London and last stay in Paris.

First visit to Kerry.

Riders to the Sea published in *Samhain*.

The Shadow of the Glen produced by the Irish National Theatre Society to hostile nationalist response.

Begins work on *The Well of the Saints*.

1904   *Riders to the Sea* produced.

The Well of the Saints finished and put into rehearsal.

Begins work on *The Playboy of the Western World*.

The Shadow of the Glen published in *Samhain*.

1905	First performance of *The Well of the Saints*, 4 Feb.; publication in London and Dublin.
	Tour of the West of Ireland with Jack B. Yeats commissioned by *Manchester Guardian*.
	Made one of the three directors of the Abbey Theatre with W.B. Yeats and Lady Gregory.
1906	Engagement to Molly Allgood, actress at the Abbey Theatre.
1907	First performance of *The Playboy*, 25 Jan., provokes riots.
	The Playboy published.
	The Aran Islands published.
	Begins work on *Deirdre of the Sorrows*.
1908	*The Tinker's Wedding* published.
	Revival of *The Well of the Saints* at the Abbey.
	Unsuccessful operation.
	Visit to Germany.
	Death of his mother.
1909	Dies, 24 March, in the Elpis nursing home in Dublin.
	Poems and Translations published.
1910	*Deirdre of the Sorrows* performed.
	Publication of the collected *Works of J.M. Synge* in 4 vols.

ABBREVIATIONS

The following is a list of abbreviated references used for the principal sources of this edition. For secondary material, see the *Critical Bibliography*.

1905 = *The Well of the Saints*, Abbey Theatre Series, Vol. I, (London: A.H. Bullen, 1905). First edition of the play.

1905 (JMS) = Synge's own copy of the first edition in which he made manuscript alterations, now in the library of Trinity College Dublin.

1905 (Quinn) = *The Well of the Saints* (New York: John Quinn, 1905). Limited copyright edition published simultaneously with the first edition.

Prompt-book = Abbey theatre typescript of *The Well of the Saints* used as prompt-book in the first production, showing theatrical alterations and including a typescript of scenes in Act III revised by Synge in 1908.

TCD MSS = Manuscript material in Trinity College Dublin, catalogued in *The Synge Manuscripts in the Library of Trinity College, Dublin* (Dublin: Dolmen Press, 1971).

Plays (1932) = *The Works of John M. Synge*, Vol. I, *Plays* (London: Allen & Unwin, 1932). First printed text to incorporate revisions of Act III of *The Well of the Saints*.

Poems = J.M. Synge, *Collected Works*, general editor, Robin Skelton, Vol. I, *Poems*, ed. Robin Skelton, (Oxford University Press, 1962).★

Prose = *Collected Works*, Vol. II, *Prose*, ed. Alan Price, (Oxford University Press, 1966).★

Plays I = *Collected Works*, Vol. III, *Plays*, Book 1, ed. Ann Saddlemyer, (Oxford University Press, 1968). Contains the text of *The Well of the Saints* with many manuscript variants and a detailed appendix concerned with the worksheets and commentary on the play.★

Plays II = *Collected Works*, Vol. IV, *Plays*, Book 2, ed. Ann Saddlemyer, (Oxford University Press, 1968).★

★Reprinted in 1982 by Colin Smythe, Gerrards Cross, Bucks., and The Catholic University of America Press, Washington, D.C.

INTRODUCTION

In his well-known Preface to the original edition of *The Well of the Saints*, W.B. Yeats gives us a dramatic version of Synge's career. The facts are less dramatic, as facts tend to be. J.M. Synge, who came from an Anglo-Irish Protestant family, *was* educated at Trinity College Dublin, and *did* spend time in Germany and France—first studying music in Würzburg before moving to Paris with the idea of a career in literature, whether as a critic or as a writer it is not clear. But Yeats's image of Synge's wandering "among people whose life is as picturesque as the Middle Ages, playing his fiddle to Italian sailors, and listening to stories in Bavarian woods" hardly fits in with what we know of Synge's soberly respectable, even sedentary residence on the Continent. The great injunction itself may not have been quite so striking as it seems in Yeats's account:

> Give up Paris. You will never create anything by reading Racine, and Arthur Symons will always be a better critic of French literature. Go to the Aran Islands. Live there as if you were one of the people themselves; express a life that has never found expression.[1]

Yeats and Synge met first in December 1896, as Synge noted in

1. W.B. Yeats, "Preface to the First Edition of *The Well of the Saints*," in *Essays and Introductions* (London, 1961), p. 299.

his diary. At that stage, it seems, so far from advising him to give up Paris and criticism, Yeats encouraged Synge to "go in for literary reviewing."[2] It seems likely that it was in February 1899, when Synge had already made his first visit to Aran the year before and had published an article about it as well as his first literary reviews, that Yeats pronounced the famous words. This date would tally with that given in the Preface and would explain how Yeats was in a position to know that Arthur Symons would "always be a better critic of French literature." The element of prophetic pronouncement in the story as Yeats tells it is removed.

And yet, though the story may not be the literal truth, it is in a very real sense significant. The visit to Aran was crucial in the development of Synge's creative imagination and in just the way Yeats suggests. Synge's early "poems and impressionistic essays" were, as Yeats describes them, "full of that kind of morbidity that has its roots in too much brooding over methods of expression, and ways of looking upon life"; before Aran, indeed, "life had cast no light into his writings."[3] In a notebook Synge described the remarkable impact of the first visit to the islands on him:

> If a man could come with a full power of appreciation and stand for the first time before a woman—a woman perhaps who was very beautiful—what would he suffer? If a man grew up knowing nothing of death or decay and found suddenly a grey corpse in his path what would [he] suffer? Some such emotion was in me the day I looked first on these rising magnificent waves towering in dazzling white and green before the cliff. (*Prose,* p. 97n.)

Aran represented for Synge an extraordinary awakening to the reality of the world. It is perhaps partly this experience which gives such imaginative feeling to Martin Doul with his new-found sight:

> it's few sees anything but them is blind for a space. It's few sees the old women rotting for the grave, and it's few sees the like of yourself [to Molly Byrne] though it's shining

---

2. So his mother reported in a letter to her son Robert in December 1897, quoted in *My Uncle John: Edward Stephens's Life of J.M. Synge,* ed. Andrew Carpenter, (Oxford, 1974), p. 109.

3. *Essays and Introductions,* p. 298. Most of Synge's early work has now been published in the *Collected Works;* see particularly *Poems* and *Prose.*

you are, like a high lamp, would drag in the ships out of the sea.

Obviously too much could be made of the transformation brought about in Synge by visiting Aran. It took him a long time—four years from his first visit in 1898 to his fifth and last in 1902—before he was able to write his first successful play. It is often forgotten that he actually used Aran only once as the setting for a play (*Riders to the Sea*) and much of the material for his work was drawn from other parts of the country: Wicklow, which he had known well since he was a boy, West Kerry and the Blasket Islands, which he visited while writing his later plays. But in Aran he first recognized images and figures to compel his imagination, and in writing *The Aran Islands* (written between 1898 and 1902, though not published until 1907) he began to find the means to express them.

Yeats's Preface also suggests the background against which Synge's career was so significant. "Irishmen have written well before Synge," declared George Moore with characteristic rhetoric, "but they have written well by casting off Ireland; but here was a man inspired by Ireland, a country that had not inspired any art since the tenth or twelfth century, a country to which it was fatal to return."[4] The main thrust of the National Literary Society (founded 1892) and the Irish Literary Theatre (1899), in both of which Yeats was the leading voice, was to turn back to Ireland for inspiration, to turn away from the cosmopolitanism and decadence of contemporary literature. Separatist nationalism obviously had a part in this: the literary movement has to be seen in the context of such diverse cultural events as the founding of the Gaelic Athletic Association (for the revival of Irish sports) in 1884 and the Gaelic League (for the revival of the Irish language) in 1893—all part of the process of emancipation from British cultural influence. But there was also the desire for new sources of literary material in place of what Yeats complains of as "that conventional language of modern poetry which has begun to make us all weary."[5] Before Synge, Douglas Hyde and Lady Gregory had started experimenting with the Anglo-Irish dialect as a literary medium, Hyde in his *Love Songs of Connacht* (1893) and Lady Gregory in *Cuchulain of Muirthemne* (1902). For George Moore, who was

---

4. George Moore, *Hail and Farewell: Vale* (London, 1914), p. 191.

5. *Essays and Introductions*, p. 298.

already an established novelist and had sampled and rejected a number of fashionable literary styles, Ireland represented "the untilled field."[6] In the ancient Irish mythology, in the language and folklore of the Irish country people, Yeats and the other writers of the revival saw the opportunity for creating a literature of renewed meaning and imaginative force.

"Live there as if you were one of the people themselves; express a life that has never found expression." The implications of Yeats's statement provided a central source for misunderstanding between the literary revivalists and their audience. For Irish nationalists, conscious of a colonial tradition in which their sense of identity had been ignored or mocked, nothing could be more laudable than "to express a life that had never found expression." "We will show," said the manifesto of the Irish Literary Theatre, "that Ireland is not the home of buffoonery and easy sentiment, as it has been represented, but the home of an ancient idealism. We are confident of the support of all Irish people, who are weary of misrepresentation."[7] From this point of view what appears above all important is that the Irish life, which had been ignored and derided, should be given its proper dignity in literature, should be expressed truly rather than in the satiric caricatures of the stage Irishman. But the allegiance of imaginative writers is ultimately to the expression rather than the life, to the truth of their own imagination rather than the truth of the experience from which it springs. Hence the gulf in understanding which appeared between the writers and their audience from the very beginning of the movement.

Yeats's *The Countess Cathleen* was one of the first plays to be put on by the Irish Literary Theatre in 1899. The story of a countess who sells her soul for gold to feed the starving Irish peasants aroused protests of sacrilege which may seem hard for us now to understand. Yeats was giving dramatic and poetic expression to what he would have regarded as a myth, and there seems an extraordinary literalism in objections to its lack of religious orthodoxy. But here, and throughout the many ensuing controversies of the Abbey Theatre, the stumbling-block was the issue of fidelity to the life of the people, or to an idealized version of that life. It is understandable if Irish men and

---

6. Moore gave this title to the collection of stories he wrote for translation into Irish as a model for Irish writers.

7. Quoted by Lady Gregory, *Our Irish Theatre* (New York, 1913), p. 9.

women, intensely proud of their loyalty to the Catholic Church, with bitter memories of Protestant efforts to proselytize under the duress of the great famine (those who changed their religion in such circumstances were called "soupers"), should have been quick to react against *The Countess of Cathleen*. Synge's own first play to be performed, *The Shadow of the Glen*, ran into the same sort of trouble. The dramatization of a folktale which Synge had actually heard on Inishmaan during his first visit to Aran, it was stigmatized in the Irish press as a slur on Irish womanhood. Synge, who could write a play in which an Irish country woman was shown in a loveless marriage, forced to leave her home with a tramp, was "utterly a stranger to the Irish character." There was in all this, of course, both class prejudice and religious feeling, deep suspicion of writers such as Yeats and Synge who came from an Anglo-Irish Protestant background. But it was ultimately a suspicion of their claims to represent truly the national experience of the people.

It was such a background which led to the explosion of feeling over *The Playboy of the Western World* in 1907. But we can see it illustrated equally, if less vociferously, in the reaction to *The Well of the Saints,* when it was first produced in 1905. From the beginning there was trouble among the company of actors—still at that stage only partly professional. One actress refused to take part unless an objectionable line was altered or removed. Frank Fay, the brother of the director and himself cast for the Saint, was "dead against" having the play performed at the opening of the company's new home, the Abbey Theatre. "He says," Synge reported, "my work is only addressed to the blasé town-dwelling theatre-goers . . . that he wants a National Theatre that will draw the people" (*Plays* I, p. xxii). The complaints of Joseph Holloway, the theatre's architect, who attended many of the play's rehearsals, are voluminously recorded in his amazing journal.[8] The following comment is fairly typical:

> Mr. J.M. Synge is a complete master of picturesque strong language of somewhat brutal coarseness, not to say sheer repulsiveness. His bump of reverence for sacred things is

---

8. Some parts of Holloway's gigantic manuscript journal, *A Dublin Play-goer's Impressions,* have been published in *Joseph Holloway's Abbey Theatre* (Carbondale, Ill., 1967), ed. Robert Hogan and Michael J. O'Neill, but quotation here is from an unpublished part of the original in the National Library of Ireland.

not strongly developed nor is his outlook of the rosy rational order—drab is his only colour when poor human nature is his model, and when he brands the creatures of his imagination with Irish names and makes them move in front of Irish scenes the reality of his characters fails to become apparent to an Irish audience.

In view of all this, it is only surprising that the negative response to *The Well of the Saints* took the fairly mild form of poor attendance and hostile reviews rather than the more violent disapproval which was to greet *The Playboy*. It cannot have helped Synge's standing with Irish nationalists that the only really appreciative reviews were from the English rather than the Irish papers.[9]

To support the charge that the plays were un-Irish, Synge's critics were eager to find foreign sources for them. Arthur Griffith, editor of *The United Irishman* and later to become the first prime minister of the Irish Free State, had claimed *The Shadow of the Glen* was derived from the decadent Latin author Petronius. The same polemical bias underlay source-hunting for *The Well of the Saints,* Griffith again denying Synge's originality: "The story—a well-known one—has been treated in our own time by an English novelist."[10] It was, however, a professed admirer of the play, George Moore, who floated the idea that *The Well of the Saints* was based on a one-act French play, Georges Clemenceau's *Le Voile de Bonheur (The Veil of Happiness)*. The suggestion was enthusiastically taken up as evidence of Synge's foreign contamination, although the similarities of Synge's play to Clemenceau's are very slight and there is no reason to believe that Synge knew *Le Voile de Bonheur*. *The Well of the Saints* is, in fact, the only one of Synge's plays which does have a non-Irish source, the fifteenth century *Moralité de l'Aveugle et du Boiteux (Morality play of the Blind Man and the Cripple)* of Andrieu de la Vigne, though this was not established

---

9. Virtually all of the Irish papers printed highly critical reviews, the extreme nationalist *Leader* (Feb. 11, 1905) and *United Irishman* (Feb. 11, 1905) being particularly virulent. In England, on the other hand, there was an admiring notice in the *Pall Mall Gazette* (Feb. 11, 1905) and a spirited defense of the play against its Irish attackers in the *Observer* (Feb. 12, 1905).

10. *United Irishman,* Feb. 11, 1905. Griffith does not name the English novelist, but Padraic Colum recalled that it was Wilkie Collins's story "Poor Miss Finch" that Griffith had in mind (*The Road Round Ireland* [New York, 1926], p. 302).

until well after Synge's death.[11] This was the second piece in a three-part presentation devised for a festival in honor of St. Martin, which Synge came across in his study of the *Histoire de théâtre en France au moyen-âge* by Petit de Julleville, whose courses he had attended at the Sorbonne. The first play in the trilogy was a *mystère*, a perfectly serious dramatization of episodes in the life of the saint. The final part was a wholly comic piece about a miller and a devil. As might be expected from this calculated pattern of descent from the sublime to the ridiculous, the *Moralité* which came in between was a mixture of the sacred and profane. A cripple and a blind man have formed a begging partnership with the blind man as legs and the cripple as eyes. The cripple is anxious to avoid the cortège of St. Martin, who has recently died, for fear of being cured. Separated on stage by a piece of crude comic business, they blunder across the procession and are both miraculously healed. The blind man goes off giving joyful thanks for the gift of sight, while the cripple curses the saint who has deprived him of his disability as a pretext for begging. The play ends happily, however, with the cripple's realization that he can always continue to pretend to be crippled, and enjoy the use of his limbs as well.

The *Moralité* scarcely seems very close to *The Well of the Saints* in mode or theme. They might appear to have little more in common than an ironic perception that the gifts of God are not gifts to everyone. Yet two elements in it, and their combination, may have appealed to Synge and supplied him with the starting-point for his play: the robust, even cynical, comedy of the beggars, and the parable-like structure of the story. In the French play there is that juxtaposition of coarse humor with a perfectly devout sense of the sacred which is so characteristic of mediaeval drama. In Synge the juxtaposition of diverse dramatic modes is put to very different effect, and given an ironic pointedness extremely unlike anything in the unselfconscious *Moralité*. But Martin Doul and Mary Doul are, to begin with at least, characterized as the same sort of comic beggars as Andrieu de la Vigne's, exploiting their disability, lying for a living. At the same time, the action in which they play their part is unique

---

11. It was established by Gertrude Schoepperle, "John Synge and 'His Old French Farce'", *North American Review*, 214 (1921), 504–513. Petit de Julleville's commentary on the *Moralité* is included in *Plays* I, Appendix C, pp. 265-7.

among Synge's works for its parable form. Synge usually began a play with a folk-tale, a myth, a story he had heard in Ireland; only in *The Well of the Saints* did he start from an idea, the idea of the beggars who prefer blindness to sight.

It was no doubt to emphasize its remoteness from the actual that Synge set it so vaguely "on the east of Ireland one or more centuries ago." This places the action back in a "once upon a time" world of fable where saints and miraculous cures may be more readily accepted. But his work on the play led Synge to give his characters and their Irish background a specific reality at odds with their story-book remoteness. If the main idea of the play came from outside Ireland, in *The Well of the Saints,* as in all Synge's other works, there is a constant use of place-names, incidents and allusions drawn from his knowledge of the Irish countryside. The Saint's "grave of the four beauties of God" Synge saw on Aran on his first visit, and in *The Aran Islands* he described the holy well near it with its miraculous water. He set the play in a Wicklow valley he knew well, and which he also used for the setting of his other two Wicklow plays. It is the valley of the small river Avonbeg which runs from the desolate beauty of Glenmalure—the glen of *The Shadow of the Glen*—down to the Meeting of the Waters, made famous in the nineteenth century by one of Thomas Moore's *Irish Melodies.* The first and third acts are set in Grianan, close to where Synge spent a summer in a rented house with his mother; an alternative title he considered for the play was *The Crossroads of Grianan.* The village near which the second act takes place is Ballinaclash, generally shortened to Clash, just two miles from Grianan. The character of Timmy the smith may have been suggested to him by a blacksmith in Clash whose name actually was Smith. Synge was not interested in topographical authenticity for its own sake: he was prepared to invent a place-name, Rathvanna, possibly by combining two real names, Rathdangan and Aughavanna. But it mattered to him that the scenes he imagined could be placed in a specific area he knew, and in successive manuscript drafts of the play, he narrowed down the references the characters make to places plausibly close to Grianan and Ballinaclash.

Yet at a larger level it is as a geography of the imagination that the play's Irish background is important. At times Synge seems to use both "the eastern world" and the "western world" ambiguously to signify at once the eastern or western part of Ireland and fairy-tale wonderlands. But through the play as a whole the poles of the east, west and south take on separate and distinct imaginative associations. The main action is set on the "east of Ireland," and though the Wicklow mountains are spectacularly beautiful, Synge chose to characterize the dreariness and drabness of the life there, particularly in the winter word-pictures of Martin Doul in the second act:

> it's a raw, beastly day we do have each day, till I do be thinking it's well for the blind, don't be seeing them gray clouds driving on the hill, and don't be looking on people with their noses red, the like of your nose, and their eyes weeping, and watering, the like of your eyes, God help you, Timmy the smith.

For the Wicklow people, Aran is somewhere far off in the west, barely known by hearsay:

> TIMMY Did ever you hear tell of a place across a bit of the sea, where there is an island, and the grave of the four beautiful saints?
>
> MARY DOUL I've heard people have walked round from the west and they speaking of that.

For the Saint, it is "a bare starving rock" appropriate, in the very extremity of its deprivation, for the mysterious blessing of God's presence in the holy water. But for the unromantic Molly Byrne it is only a backward area—"that wild place, where, I'm told, there are no decent houses, or fine-looking people at all." The south is the country of Martin Doul's imagination, a country of escape. In Act II it is the world into which he projects his fantasy of a sensuous life with Molly Byrne:

> Let you come on now, I'm saying, to the lands of Iveragh and the Reeks of Cork, where you won't set down the width of your two feet and not be crushing fine flowers, and making sweet smells in the air .

At the end of the play it offers a refuge from the hostility of the villagers: "we're going on the two of us to the towns of the south, where the people will have kind voices maybe, and we won't know their bad looks or their villainy at all." East, west and south represent images of life associated with the villagers, the Saint and the blind beggars, and the structure and meaning of *The Well of the Saints* is developed from the interplay of the three.

W.G. Fay complained that "every character in the play from the Saint to Timmy the Smith was bad-tempered right through the play," but Synge said that he wanted to write "like a monochrome painting, all in shades of one colour."[12] It is hardly accurate that all the characters are consistently bad-tempered, but certainly few of them are very obviously sympathetic. This is particularly true of the ordinary people of the village, though Timmy the smith might seem a partial exception. By Synge's own account, he is "a good-natured, naive, busy-body with a hot temper" (*Plays* I, p. xxiii). The good nature is apparent in the uneasy compassion he feels at the coming disillusionment of Martin Doul in Act I: "God help him. . . . What will he be doing when he sees his wife this day?" It is the same good nature which he himself proclaims loudly in Act III, but by then we can see its insensitive officiousness: "The saint's come to marry the two of us, and I'm after speaking a word for yourselves, the way he'll be curing you now, for if you're a foolish man itself, I do be pitying you, for I've a kind heart, when I think of you sitting dark again, and you after seeing a while, and working for your bread." Molly Byrne is altogether a more unpleasant character and Synge must have smiled inwardly at Fay's suggestion that she "might be made a lovable young girl" by way of redressing the imbalance of bad temper in the play. Her frivolous fooling with Martin Doul and the Saint's cloak verges sufficiently close on sacrilege to worry Timmy; it is her rebuff to Martin when he mistakes her for his wife—"Let you keep away from me, and not be soiling my chin"—which leads the crowd from embarrassment into jeering mockery. More cruel than anything else in the play are the terms of her rejection of Martin Doul's wooing which she has at least half invited:

> Go off now after your wife, and if she beats you again, let you go after the tinker girls is above running the hills, or down among the sluts of the town, and you'll learn one day, maybe, the way a man should speak with a well-reared civil girl the like of me.

Giving force and depth to the sexual humiliation of these lines is the class-based contempt of the "well-reared civil girl" for the beggar.

---

12. Quoted in E.H. Mikhail (ed.), *J.M. Synge: Interviews and Recollections* (London, 1977), p. 31.

When the play opens the pretense that Martin and Mary are beauties is a long-established fiction and Synge never gives us occasion to speculate on how it arose. But it would be consistent with the village community as we see it to think of the pretense as originating in a mixed impulse of joking and pity. There is a grotesque amusement in the spectacle of the blind beggars preening themselves on their good looks which the villagers no doubt enjoyed, yet they are aware also of the "great joy and pride" they give to Martin and Mary by maintaining the illusion. They are not naturally cruel people (with the possible exception of Molly) yet capable of cruelty as a group because of the limitations in their capacity for understanding or reflection. The neutrality of indifference can be turned into aggressive hostility by a challenge to their ordinary world. The cured beggars disturb them into self-consciousness:

> it's a queer thing the way yourself and Mary Doul are after
> setting every person in this place, and up beyond to
> Rathvanna, talking of nothing, and thinking of nothing,
> but the way they do be looking in the face. It's the devil's
> work you're after doing with your talk of fine looks.

The violent expulsion of Martin and Mary at the end is a measure of the villagers' sense of threat: "It'd be an unlucky fearful thing, I'm thinking to have the like of that man living near us at all."

The villagers' lack of understanding extends to the Saint as well as to Martin and Mary. They see him in their own terms rather than his. Molly is contemptuous because "he'd walk by the finest woman in Ireland, I'm thinking, and not trouble to raise his two eyes to look upon her face." Timmy the smith sees in him a fine body wasted: "and he a fine, brave man if it wasn't for the fasting." There is blank incomprehension of the Saint's holiness and its importance in his capacity to cure:

> It'd be a fine thing if some one in this place could pray the
> like of him, for I'm thinking the water from our own
> blessed well would do rightly if a man knew the way to be
> saying prayers.

It is a matter of a magical *abracadabra* which anyone could learn. The villagers put up what is not much more than an outward show of respect in the Saint's presence; as Synge made clear in a note for the director, "a marked difference of voice and bearing should be felt when the saint goes into church and the people are left to themselves" (*Plays* I, p. xxiii). All in all, the predominantly Catholic audience at the Abbey in 1905 might well have had some reason to complain if they thought that Synge intended the villagers to be representative of ordinary Irish people in their attitude to religion.

In the character of the Saint there was less to give offense, though he is not by any means an orthodox figure. Synge, in fact, seems deliberately to have left an element of vagueness in the conception of the Saint and his status. In the list of characters he is described as "a wandering friar" and this might suggest that "saint" is used only loosely to describe someone whose life is devoted to religion. This impression was cultivated in the first production where fear of appearing sacrilegious led to alterations in the text: instead of "a saint of the Almighty God," for instance, he was introduced as "a man the like of the saints of God." Yet presumably with the *Moralité,* concerned with St. Martin, as a starting-point, Synge did originally think in terms of a real saint, performing such miracles as are required for canonization. He gives to the Saint at one point lines paraphrased from the old Irish hymn known as St. Patrick's Breastplate:

> you'd do well to be thinking on the way sin has brought
> blindness to the world, and to be saying a prayer for your
> own sakes against false prophets and heathens, and the
> words of women and smiths, and all knowledge that
> would soil the soul or the body of a man.

This is not necessarily to identify the Saint as Patrick himself, but it makes the association.

In a letter to Lady Gregory during rehearsals Synge reported that "Colum finds my play unsatisfactory because the Saint is really a Protestant!" (*Plays* I, p. xxii). Although that is hardly the case, we can perhaps see what Padraic Colum meant. Synge came from a staunchly Church of Ireland family with an evangelical tradition against which he reacted quite early on; by the age of sixteen or seventeen he had more or less lost his faith. It was difficult for him to accept emotionally or respond sympathetically to any form of devout Christian belief, and because of his Protestant background particularly difficult with Catholicism. There is very little allusion to religious practice and belief in his account of the people in *The Aran Islands,* and where Synge does comment on them it is often to detect signs of an older underlying paganism. But it is clear that in the Saint he tried to create an impressive spokesman for the spiritual life, one whom he himself could respect and admire. In early drafts of the play the Saint was an uninspired sermonizer, and it was to lend him dignity and eloquence that Synge developed the major speech which closes the first act:

May the Lord who has given you sight send a little sense into your heads, the way it won't be on your two selves you'll be looking—on two pitiful sinners of the earth—but on the splendour of the Spirit of God, you'll see an odd time shining out through the big hills, and steep streams falling to the sea.

There is a suggestion of pantheism here, of the worship of the Deity through nature, which Synge himself, an ardent nature-lover, would have found more sympathetic than any orthodox Christian creed.

The Saint's vision is impressive in its austere asceticism, especially against the background of the small-minded villagers. And yet the gap between his and their understanding of life is a measure of his limitation as well as theirs. His ascetic idealism has little relation to the reality of the world he lives in. He can have no conception of the ordinary materialism of such as Timmy the smith with his pride in his new "house with four rooms in it above on the hill." Nothing underlines the Saint's lack of touch with reality more effectively than a throwaway line of Mary Doul in the first act. Molly Byrne explains that she and Bride have been entrusted with the Saint's bell, cloak and holy water—

for young girls, says he, are the cleanest holy people you'd see walking the world.

MARY DOUL [sits down, laughing to herself] Well, the saint's a simple fellow, and it's no lie.

Even before we meet him, that judgment stands: the man who believes in the automatic holiness and chastity of such as Molly Byrne is a "simple fellow" to the point of foolishness. From early on in the play, therefore, the Saint's vision is ironically called in question by the ordinary reality of the villagers' lives against which it is set. The dynamic of the action is to take us through to the climax of the third act in which that idealist attitude of the Saint meets the challenge of a formal antagonist in Martin Doul with his alternative "vision" of the world.

Synge took great pains not to sentimentalize the blind beggars and their situation. Nothing would have been easier, or more intolerable, than a pathetic image of the couple cherishing their beautiful illusion. The play opens in an ironic minor key with the tone of the relationship that of mild marital squabbling, rather than any more eye-catching form of happiness. The illusion of beauty is comic rather than pathetic in the complacent words of Mary Doul:

> I've heard tell there isn't anything like the wet south wind does be blowing upon us, for keeping a white beautiful skin—the like of my skin—on your neck and on your brows, and there isn't anything at all like a fine skin for putting splendour on a woman.

We are made aware of the inversion of the blind viewpoint— "the seeing is a queer lot, and you'd never know the thing they'd do." We are not encouraged to identify with the plight of the beggars as outsiders but rather observe with detached amusement their self-satisfied contempt and distrust for the "seeing rabble below." Initially at least, ours is an ironic vantage-point on the home-made world of their own in which Martin and Mary live.

However, a common strategy in Synge's drama is to set up a comic perspective and then to shift the mode of the drama away from comedy. Such a shift is central to *The Well of the Saints*. The comedian habitually distances us from feeling, suspends our capacity for sharing pain or suffering. Such a technique of ironic distance is there in the opening scenes of *The Well of the Saints,* never more than in the gallows humor of Martin and Mary's speculations on the "wonder" Timmy has promised them.

> Maybe they're hanging a thief above at the bit of a tree? I'm told it's a great sight to see a man hanging by his neck, but what joy would that be to ourselves, and we not seeing it at all?

But as the prospect of their cure approaches, we find ourselves no longer immune from sympathy; our detachment is eroded. In this development of discomfort the scene with Molly and the girls is crucial. In the context of Molly's heartless and inane mockery of Martin in the Saint's cloak, the beggars take on a new dignity:

MOLLY BYRNE . . . Isn't that a fine holy-looking
saint, Timmy the smith? *[Laughing foolishly.]* There's a
grand handsome fellow, Mary Doul, and if you seen him
now, you'd be as proud, I'm thinking, as the archangels
below, fell out with the Almighty God.

MARY DOUL *[with quiet confidence going to* MARTIN
DOUL *and feeling his cloak]* It's proud we'll be this day
surely.

The foolish laughter of Molly is laughter we cannot share and
our feelings go out to the vulnerability of Martin and Mary.

While at work on the play, Synge drew up a plan showing
the changing mode of its various parts, and the final scene of
Act I he marked "tragic" (see *Plays* I, Appendix C, p. 264). It is
the more tragic because of the moment of ecstasy which follows
Martin's cure. A dramatic off-stage cry breaks into the aimless
arguments of the villagers—"Oh, glory be to God, I see now
surely. . . . I see the walls of the church, and yourself, holy
father, and the great width of the sky." There is a terrible tragic
irony in the words of wondering delight with which he greets
Molly Byrne, mistaking her for his wife:

Oh, it was no lie they told me, Mary Doul. Oh, glory to
God and the seven saints I didn't die and not see you at all.
The blessing of God on the water, and the feet carried it
round through the land, for it's grand hair you have *[she
lowers her head a little confused],* and soft skin, and eyes
would make the saints, if they were dark awhile and seeing
again, fall down out of the sky.

The people's reaction is one of painful embarrassment and it is
to escape the intolerable burden of sympathy that they join in
the jeering taunts as Martin searches ever more desperately for
Mary in a cruel game of ex-blind-man's-buff. By the time she
appears, cured in her turn, they have hardened themselves to
laugh at the beggars' mutual disillusionment. The slanging-
match which follows, with all its grotesque hyperbole, could in
fact almost be comic, were it not for the intensity of feeling
which it expresses. Martin and Mary take their tragedy trag-
ically. Anyone can be hurt and humiliated; only a few can make
of that humiliation a significant betrayal.

Yet the move from comedy to tragedy is never made once
and irrevocably in a Synge play. After the dramatic moment of
tragic loss at the end of the first act, Martin is once again seen in

a comic light at the beginning of the second. Like the traditional comic beggar, he has little enthusiasm for hard labor, and there is a splendid vituperative edge to his grumbles at his taskmaster, Timmy the smith, who insists on his stripping off for work:

> Oh, God help me! [*He begins taking off his coat.*] I've heard tell you stripped the sheet from your wife and you putting her down into the grave, and there isn't the like of you for plucking your living ducks, the short days, and leaving them running round in their skins, in the great rains and the cold.

It is a sour sort of comedy, with Martin's disillusioned view of reality lending gloom to the atmosphere, and yet there is a real humor in the contrast between the hard-working smith intent on his business and the lazy self-pitying ex-beggar.

It may seem astonishing to modern readers that reviewers of the first production of *The Well of the Saints* found in it evidence of Synge's obsession with sex. Yet for Dublin in 1905, the treatment of Martin Doul's feeling for Molly Byrne must have appeared shockingly explicit. Already in the first act we are given a glimpse of his fantasies about her:

> she's a sweet beautiful voice you'd never tire to be hearing, if it was only the pig she'd be calling, or crying out in the long grass, maybe, after her hens. [*Speaking pensively.*] It should be a fine soft, rounded woman, I'm thinking, would have a voice the like of that.

Molly is aware of her attractiveness—she is aware of little else—and when she finds herself alone with Martin Doul in Act II she flirts with him automatically without taking him seriously for a moment. She has not the slightest understanding of the significance of Martin's vision of her.

> MARTIN DOUL . . . You'd do right, I'm saying, not to marry a man is after looking out a long while on the bad days of the world, for what way would the like of him have fit eyes to look on yourself, when you rise up in the morning and come out of the little door you have above in the lane, the time it'd be a fine thing if a man would be seeing, and losing his sight, the way he'd have your two eyes facing him, and he going the roads, and shining above him, and he looking in the sky, and springing up from the earth, the time he'd lower his head, in place of the muck that seeing men do meet all roads spread on the world.

MOLLY BYRNE [*who has listened half mesmerized, starting away*] It's the like of that talk you'd hear from a man would be losing his mind.

The lunatic, the lover and the poet are of imagination all compact, and the imagination which Molly takes to be that of the madman is that of the lover/poet. Only the lover has "fit eyes" to see the beloved; only the poet has the words to express what he sees.

The second act ends like the first in humiliation for Martin, a humiliation if anything more intense because more intimately personal. The renewed blindness which comes on at the very moment when Mary Doul enters and the outraged Molly Byrne turns on him makes for a moment of terrible depth and anguish.

MARTIN DOUL [*turns round, sees* MARY DOUL, *whispers to* MOLLY BYRNE *with imploring agony*] Let you not put shame on me, Molly, before herself and the smith. Let you not put shame on me, and I after saying fine words to you, and dreaming . . . dreams . . . in the night. [*He hesitates, and looks round the sky.*] Is it a storm of thunder is coming, or the last end of the world? [*He staggers towards* MARY DOUL, *tripping slightly over tin can.*] The heavens is closing, I'm thinking, with darkness and great trouble passing in the sky. [*He reaches* MARY DOUL, *and seizes her left arm with both his hands—with a frantic cry.*] Is it the darkness of thunder is coming, Mary Doul? Do you see me clearly with your eyes?

MARY DOUL [*snatches her arm away, and hits him with empty sack across the face*] I see you a sight too clearly, and let you keep off from me now.

Molly's shaming of him represents the destruction of his world, the fantasy-world of his imagination of which she was the center. The apocalyptic imagery gives resonance to a return to blindness which is more than merely physical. With Mary Doul's fierce rejection, Martin's isolation is complete.

All three acts of *The Well of the Saints* have a similar movement: beginning on the level of detached ironic comedy, the action develops to a point of all but complete identification with the protagonists. At the start of Act III, as with the opening scenes of the other acts, we are back in a predominantly comic mode. Martin's "soliloquy," overheard by Mary Doul, makes for a moment of broad humor when he tries to flee in terror:

> Oh, merciful God, set my foot on the path this day, and I'll
> be saying prayers morning and night, and not straining my
> ear after young girls, or doing any bad thing till I die—
> MARY DOUL [*indignantly*] Let you not be telling lies to
> the Almighty God.

However, the reunion between the two in which they rebuild their relationship on the basis of a new illusion is one of the most subtle and delicate scenes in the play in its combination of irony and understanding. Mary and Martin must each find their own means to a restored self-belief before they can meet on equal terms. Martin is admiring when Mary announces the fiction of her long white hair, but she ruthlessly refuses to help him towards a similar fiction:

> MARTIN DOUL [*taking off his hat and feeling his head,
> speaking with hesitation*] Did you think to look, Mary Doul,
> would there be a whiteness the like of that coming upon
> me?
> MARY DOUL [*with extreme contempt*] On you, God
> help you? . . . In a short while you'll have a head on you as
> bald as an old turnip you'd see rolling round in the muck.

There is no quarter given in this battle of competing egos, and it is only when Martin discovers the possibilities of a long white beard to match Mary's long white hair that mutual satisfaction is achieved.

The return to illusion on the part of the beggars has met with stern disapproval from some critics who feel that Synge could not have endorsed such escapism.[13] But the play is not conceived in the black and white moralistic terms of truth and its opposite. Martin and Mary are to some extent professional liars: "a priest itself," says Martin, "would believe the lies of an old man would have a fine white beard growing on his chin." When Martin congratulates Mary on her discovery, it is with admiration for her inventiveness: "you're a cute thinking woman, Mary Doul, and it's no lie." What they create with their new vision of beauty is something midway between the conscious lies they tell priests and passers-by and their former illusion in which they fully believed. They know at some level that it is false, as we can see when they are threatened with sight

---

13. For example, Donna Gerstenberger, *John Millington Synge* (New York, 1964), p. 55.

again: "what good'll our gray hairs be itself, if we have our sight, the way we'll see them falling each day, and turning dirty in the rain?" Yet Synge demands our sympathetic feeling for the need for this degree of illusory self-respect. As Martin and Mary enjoy the spring sounds and smells of the countryside, there is a real and moving suggestion of emotional renewal.

It is for this reason that the prospect of a second cure seems to us, as to them, persecution by the Saint and the villagers. We feel for them in their pathetic and hopeless attempts to hide themselves away. In the opening scene of the play the beggars' suspicion of the sighted was viewed as comic inversion— "they're a bad lot those that have their sight"—but now they seem justified: "the lot of them young girls, the devil save them, have sharp terrible eyes, would pick out a poor man I'm thinking, and he lying below hid in his grave." The deepest irony of all is that, to express their dissent from the values of the Saint and the villagers, they have only the language in which those values are implicit. "The Lord protect us from the saints of God," cries Mary Doul. Synge often gave comic pointing to the miscellaneous Irish invocation of the Deity, most strikingly, of course, with Christy's confession in *The Playboy*—

PEGEEN Is it killed your father?

CHRISTY With the help of God I did surely—

but nowhere more significantly than here. Who but the Lord *is* there to rescue Martin and Mary from the blessing of sight brought by His saint? They are caught uncertainly between prayer and blasphemy: "who'd know rightly if it's good words or bad would save us this day from himself?"

Everything in the play builds towards the climax of the second attempted cure by the Saint. It was the scene Synge worked hard to revise for the revival of the play in 1908 and which he most wanted to see well performed in the theatre. His aim in the revisions was to add depth and clarity to both the Saint's arguments and Martin's, and to orchestrate the reactions of the people. He was conscious of the dangers of the Saint appearing an unsympathetic preacher and he added a stage direction to suggest a more kindly tone in his eloquent speech to Martin.

SAINT *[coming close to* MARTIN DOUL *and putting his hand on his shoulder]* Did you never hear tell of the summer and the fine spring in places where the holy men of Ireland

have built up churches to the Lord, that you'd wish to be
closed up and seeing no sight of the glittering seas, and the
furze is opening above, will soon have the hills shining as if
it was fine creels of gold they were, rising to the sky?

But equally he took great care with Martin's alternative blind
man's vision:

I'll say it's ourselves have finer sight than the lot of you,
and we sitting abroad in the sweetness of the warmth of
night [SAINT *draws back from him*] hearing a late thrush,
maybe, and the swift flying things do be racing in the air,
till we do be looking up in our own minds into a grand
sky, and seeing lakes and broadening rivers and hills are
waiting for the spade and plough.

The crowd's reaction at first is one of more or less neutral
enjoyment of the dispute, but as Martin definitively rejects the
Saint's offer of sight, they become more aggressive. The suggestion that Mary should be cured and Martin left blind is in
some sense an attack on him, as he himself feels: "Would you
have her looking on me and saying hard words to me till the
hour of death?" They will not tolerate the idea of the couple
deliberately remaining blind.

If it's choosing a wilful blindness you are, there isn't
anyone will give you a hap'worth of meal, or be doing the
little things you do need to keep you living in the world at
all.

They put forward shrewd arguments to tempt Mary to forsake
Martin and accept her sight. When revising the scene, Synge
steadily increased the violence of the people's reaction against
Martin and gave them lines enthusiastically dragging him away
at the Saint's bidding: "That's it. That's it. Come forward till
we drop him in the pool beyond." With Martin's final blatant
and scandalous defiance of orthodoxy in the spilling of the holy
water, they are prepared to stone the beggars out of the village.

The ordinary people's reality in *The Well of the Saints* lives
between two worlds of imagination, that of Martin and Mary
on the one hand, and of the Saint on the other. The Saint insists
that if one has the vision to see "the Spirit of God . . . shining
out through the big hills, and steep streams falling to the sea,"
then the body can be forgotten, ignored. His is an aesthetic
which glorifies the poor, the mean, the underfed as the in-
heritors of spiritual grace; it is the spirit of the Sermon on the

Mount. But the Saint makes little contact with an everyday world of reality, with the Timmy the smiths and the Molly Byrnes, who do value strength of body, beauty, comfort. These *are* their realities. The inner life of imagination of the blind beggars is constructed by an interiorization of these ordinary realities. Their values are those of Timmy and Molly; they have no more time for the humble pride of spiritual self-abnegation than the villagers have. But their passionate egotism in clinging to the illusion of vanity separates them from those whose sensibilities are deadened by daily contact with the ugliness and superficiality of the actual. They set new standards for self-satisfaction—impossible standards which trouble because they cannot be satisfied. They re-make, and then Martin has fiercely to defend, their imaginary life. They reject the Saint's ascetic vision because what it means in fact is living with the reality of the Timmys and Mollys.

> What was it I seen my first day, but your own bleeding feet
> and they cut with the stones, and my last day, but the
> villainy of herself you're wedding, God forgive you, to
> Timmy the smith.

It would be possible to give a schematic interpretation of *The Well of the Saints* in terms of three sorts of vision: the ordinary vision of the villagers, the spiritual vision of the Saint, and the poetic vision of Martin Doul. But though the play has its origins in parable, its dramatic images are not reducible to this sort of abstract pattern. The mood and meaning of the final scene, for instance, work by implicit suggestion rather than any direct symbolic significance. As the beggars leave, with the violent hostility of the crowd, Synge is careful to qualify the tone of defiant triumph in Martin's speeches with more skeptical views. Mary goes off with him to the south, but without his enthusiasm:

> MARY DOUL *[despondingly]* That's the truth, surely,
> and we'd have a right to be gone, if it's a long way
> itself, where you do have to be walking with a slough of
> wet on the one side and a slough of wet on the other, and
> you going a stony path with a north wind blowing behind.

Even more disturbing, because of its very casualness, is Timmy's remark after they leave:

> There's a power of deep rivers with floods in them where
> you do have to be lepping the stones and you going to the

south, so I'm thinking the two of them will be drowned
together in a short while, surely.

Do the beggars go out to an almost certain death, or is this only
a callous parting shot from Timmy, a brutal good riddance?
T.R. Henn comments in words which brilliantly suggest the
ambiguity of the play's effect:

> Synge's reticence gives no symbolism, as a lesser poet
> might have done, to sloughs or rivers or winds. Only what
> Martin creates will—for this verbal moment—remain; for
> here illusions can be recreated, and perhaps maintained, in
> the gallant security of blindness.[14]

The first production of *The Well of the Saints* was non-
naturalistic in *décor,* and this may have contributed to its lack of
success. Although the Abbey Theatre was to become associated
with so-called peasant naturalism, the theatre movement in
origin was partly a reaction against the naturalistic style. Both
Yeats and Synge opposed those who wanted to follow the lead
of Ibsen, then thought of exclusively as the founder of naturalistic social drama. In his Preface to *The Well of the Saints* Yeats
describes, with evident approval, the *mise en scène:*

> While I write, we are rehearsing *The Well of the Saints,* and
> are painting for it decorative scenery, mountains in one or
> two flat colours and without detail, ash-trees and red
> salleys with something of recurring pattern in their woven
> boughs.[15]

It is amusing to contrast Joseph Holloway's much more jaun-
diced account:

> the scenery is novel . . . The red flame-like trees for
> sidewings, and the red glow of light arising from behind a
> stone wall on to the back cloth gave the opening and
> closing scene the effect of a 'demon scene' in a pantomime
> so far was the scheme removed from nature, while the
> second scene—a harmony in gray resembling a Whistler
> nocturne—was more peculiar than convincing. The entire
> background being one work of unrelieved gray reflected a
> double shadow of each performer and had a very dis-
> tracting effect on the vision.[16]

14. T.R. Henn (ed.), *The Plays and Poems of J.M. Synge* (London, 1963),
p. 56.

15. *Essays and Introductions,* p. 305.

16. *A Dublin Playgoer's Impressions* ms., Feb. 3, 1905.

It is hardly surprising that this subtle and ironic play, with its unidealistic portrayal of Irish peasant characters and its experimental production, should not have pleased its first audiences. Most of them simply voted with their feet and stayed away.

The play won some praise, however, from George Moore among others, and an article about it in French by a friend of Synge's, Henri Lebeau, led to an approach from a German translator, Max Meyerfeld. Meyerfeld's version, *Der Heilige Brunnen,* was published and produced in Max Reinhardt's Deutsches Theater in Berlin in 1906, and though the production was not a success, it gave Synge the status of a European reputation. The play was revived in the Abbey in 1908 and it was for this production that Synge revised the final act. He was directing the play himself when he fell ill and had to go into the hospital for the operation which led to the discovery that his condition for Hodgkin's disease was incurable. He had in fact less than a year to live. It may be that, owing to his absence in the final weeks of rehearsals, the company under Lady Gregory's direction toned down the play's astringency. At least this is what one might gather from the testimony of Joseph Holloway, who thought the revival much more palatable than the original production:

> The wild beast nature of 'Martin Doul' was artistically kept
> in check, and it made him a far more agreeable personage.
> W.G. Fay made him a very repulsive old man over-
> whelmed in sensuality. Arthur Sinclair made him more of a
> dreamer with a longing for the beautiful . . . In fact, the
> play was lifted out of reality into the realm of fancy where
> it should have been from the first.[17]

This sounds like a sentimentalized version of the play.

The Well of the Saints has continued on and off in the repertoire of the Abbey Theatre with revivals about once every ten years, but it has never been as popular as some of Synge's other works. A 1969 production, directed by Hugh Hunt, transferred to London; the play was most recently performed at the Abbey in 1979 in an experimental production directed by the playwright Thomas Murphy which had only rather mixed reviews. It was surprisingly widely translated quite early on. Apart from the Meyerfeld translation in German, it was produced in Dutch in 1912, and an adaptation in Japanese was

17. *Joseph Holloway's Abbey Theatre,* p. 53.

performed and published in 1914.[18] More recently an Arabic translation was performed in Lebanon.[19] The Abbey company took the play to London in 1905 and to America on their tour in 1911. The play has since been performed from time to time in London and New York, but not apparently in a major production or in a large theatre. Theatre directors are pragmatic people, and there is no doubt that one reason for the play's neglect is that it is too short to fill an evening performance on its own. It was written between *Riders to the Sea* and *The Playboy,* Synge's two best-known plays, and it has tended to be eclipsed by them. The obvious theatrical merits of *Riders* with its stark and powerful tragic form, and *The Playboy* with its richness of comic language, may have led potential directors to undervalue the more ironic and understated dramatic images of *The Well of the Saints.*[20]

Something similar may be said of the play's critical history. There are scores of articles on *The Playboy* and *Riders* to a handful on *The Well of the Saints.* The texts of the two well-known plays have been reprinted in any number of anthologies of modern drama; *The Well of the Saints* has apparently been anthologized only once.[21] The play *has* won appreciation, sometimes from unlikely sources. Daniel Corkery, in *Synge and Anglo-Irish Literature,* written to advance a polemical nationalist thesis, could yet see the imaginative distinction of *The Well of the Saints.*[22] But in general studies of Synge's work it has often been relatively neglected. One critic sees it as Synge's first unsatisfactory attempt at a three-act play;[23] another allows that

18. The Dutch translation by L. Simons was published as *De Heiligebron* in Amsterdam in 1912, and the adaptation in Japanese by Shoyo Tsubouchi appeared as *Reigen* in Tokyo in 1914.

19. See Ghassan Maleh, "Synge in the Arab World," in *Sunshine and the Moon's Delight,* ed. S.B. Bushrui (Gerrards Cross, Bucks. & Beiruit, 1972), pp. 245-52.

20. As this goes to press, a new production is planned by the Irish Theatre Company to tour Ireland in repertoire with Yeats's *On Baile's Strand* and Beckett's *Waiting for Godot.* The juxtaposition with Yeats and Beckett should provide an illuminating context for the play.

21. In *Makers of the Modern Theatre,* ed. Barry Ulanov, (New York, 1961), pp. 238-58.

22. Daniel Corkery, *Synge and Anglo-Irish Literature* (Dublin and Cork, 1931), p. 153.

23. Donna Gerstenberger, *John Millington Synge,* p. 55.

it has "moments of great power" but claims that it is very uneven.[24] The perfunctory treatment given to *The Well of the Saints* in many such instances is visibly due to the writer's haste to get on to the rich field of controversy offered by *The Playboy*. But there have been several critics who have given the play its share of respectful attention and appreciation. Alan Price, for instance, who is concerned with the tension between drama and actuality in all of Synge's work, naturally sees *The Well of the Saints* as an important expression of that theme.[25] In fact, a problem with much of the criticism of the play has been its tendency to focus almost exclusively on thematic interpretation. The argument has turned on ideas rather than dramatic significance, and the attempt has been to puzzle out where Synge himself stood on the relation between imaginative illusion and reality. Robin Skelton sees in the play Synge's "belief in individualism, his distrust of conventional idealism, his relish of those that stand up for their right to their vision."[26] Weldon Thornton disagrees: "In the severe, static, disjunction between idea and reality we see in Martin and Mary Doul, Synge is showing that some persons do have an amazing capacity to ignore the imperative that our ideas and our experiences should be consonant."[27] This sort of debate on the rival claims of dream and reality fails to take into account the multiple nature of reality as it is dramatized in the play.

Katharine Worth has highlighted the Beckettian features of *The Well of the Saints*[28] and, partly because of Beckett, we are now in a better position to appreciate the achievement of the play. At least the example of Beckett and his immense current prestige may make readers and audiences of *The Well of the Saints* understand features of it which formerly impeded appreciation. We no longer need to apologize for a drama of inaction, in which the two central characters spend most of the play merely talking. We no longer expect dramatic characters to be obviously "sympathetic": we are unlikely to complain with

24. Raymond Williams, *Drama from Ibsen to Brecht* (London, 1968), p. 134.

25. Alan Price, *Synge and Anglo-Irish Drama* (London, 1961).

26. Robin Skelton, *The Writings of J.M. Synge* (London, 1971), p. 101.

27. Weldon Thornton, *J.M. Synge and the Western Mind* (Gerrards Cross, Bucks., 1979), p. 133.

28. Katharine Worth, *The Irish Drama of Europe from Yeats to Beckett* (London, 1978), p. 134.

W.G. Fay that everybody in *The Well of the Saints* is bad-tempered. We are accustomed to mixed modes of drama in which traditional patterns of comedy or farce are transmuted into images of anguish and despair. Yet a knowledge of Beckett may help, by contrast as well as similarity, to show us the essential sanity and objectivity of Synge in *The Well of the Saints*. Though much of his own emotion went into the creation of Martin Doul as a powerful spokesman for the imagination, he remained aware that the imagination is at once truth and illusion. And, while he refused to condemn the blind beggars as solipsist dreamers, he recognized the substantial reality of competing views of life, those of the villagers and the Saint. The distinction and originality of *The Well of the Saints* is that it reaches so deeply into the nature of what it is to see and what it is to imagine; it presents, instead of the ordinary dualism of truth and illusion, a serio-comic vision of the world which is deeply committed and yet ironically detached.

NOTE ON THE TEXT

The Well of the Saints was first published by A.H. Bullen in London and Dublin in February 1905, as Volume I of the Abbey Theatre Series of plays. A full bibliographical description can be found in Frances-Jane French, *The Abbey Theatre Series of Plays—A Bibliography* (Dublin, 1969). A limited edition to protect American copyright was simultaneously published by John Quinn in New York. The Quinn edition, however, seems to have been set from uncorrected proofs of the Bullen text and therefore has no separate authority. There were two other issues of the play in 1905, one by Maunsel in Dublin and another more expensive one, which included the Preface by W.B. Yeats, from Bullen in London. However these, and a further issue by Maunsel in 1907, are unrevised impressions of the first 1905 text. The first edition, therefore, has been chosen as the main copy-text for the present edition, as there was no later printed text which Synge would have had an opportunity to revise.

However, Synge altered the play in production and there are several manuscript sources for these alterations to be considered. The first is the bound typescript copy of the play, now in the National Library of Ireland, which was used as the prompt-book for the first production at the Abbey Theatre. It shows extensive minor emendations, cuts and theatrical revisions, as well as the detail of stage movement. Although W.G. Fay was the play's director, Synge was closely involved with the rehearsals and some (though not all) of the manuscript alterations in the prompt-book are in his hand. The second source for Synge's theatrical changes to the text is his own copy of the 1905 first edition, now in the Trinity College, Dublin, Library, into which he copied some of the prompt-book alterations. When the play was revived in 1908, Synge substantially revised a part of the third act from Martin Doul's speech to the Saint beginning *We're not asking our sight, holy father* down to the moment at which the holy water is spilled. There are two typescript versions of this revised scene, both of them almost certainly typed by Synge: the first, which has many manuscript changes, in the Trinity College collection, the second and later one with the National Library prompt-book.

Attempts to incorporate these theatrical changes have made for variation in some of the printed texts published since Synge's death. The edition of the *Plays* published by Allen & Unwin in 1932, apparently prepared by Edward H. Synge, the dramatist's nephew, included the 1908 revision of the third act. The Note at the end of the volume explains that this revision was taken from "the Abbey Theatre's copy of the play," that is to say the prompt-book, but it is not quite clear just what version was being followed, as the text printed in 1932 is marginally different from the typescript of the revised scene now with the prompt-book. Edward Synge did not feel justified in incorporating any of the other changes in the prompt-book itself, and he apparently did not consult Synge's own copy of the first edition. In the text published in *Collected Works* in 1968 (*Plays* I), edited by Ann Saddlemyer, the alterations in Synge's own copy of the first edition are noted and, for the most part, adopted. However, Professor Saddlemyer did not have access to the prompt-book or the accompanying typescript of the 1908 revision, and therefore followed the earlier Trinity College version for the revised scene.

The present edition has new authority in so far as it is the first to make use of all the main sources of theatrical revisions of the 1905 text. The basic principle which has been adopted is to accept only those changes recorded in the prompt-book which are confirmed in Synge's copy of the first edition. Other substantial changes recorded in the prompt-book are noted, but have not been incorporated in the text. There is one exception to this general principle. A line of Timmy the smith in the second act aroused considerable protest during rehearsals: Mary Doul is described as *going by the way you'd see a priest going where there'd be a drunken man in the side ditch talking with a girl.* When Synge was first tackled about this line, he refused point-blank to alter it, insisting that the simile derived from something he had actually seen. (See *Plays* I, p. xxiv). It was only at the dress-rehearsal stage after more complaints, that it was changed, as Joseph Holloway noted in his journal, to *the way you'd see a sainted lady going where there'd be drunken people in the side ditch singing to themselves.* Although this version is recorded in Synge's own hand both in the prompt-book and in his copy of the first edition, it has been rejected in the present text as a forced bowdlerization. For the revised scene of Act III, the typescript with the prompt-book has been followed. The notes record all substantive variations from the 1905 text, but no attempt has been made to refer to manuscript variants in the considerable body of worksheets for the play in the Trinity College collection and elsewhere, as these are extensively documented in *Plays* I.

Synge appears to have punctuated on a rhythmical rather than grammatical or syntactical principle. With his special oral dialect, he tended to avoid more formal punctuation: semi-colons, for instance, he almost never uses. The largely rhythmic pointing of the first edition has been preserved in this text. Changes have been adopted only where there are clear mistakes, or where the punctuation in the prompt-book seems to offer a better pattern of intonation. Such changes are not recorded in the notes. The flow of Synge's poetic periods is so important that it seems better to keep his light punctuation, at the risk of occasional difficulty to the reader, than to tidy it up and disturb the rhythms he intended.

NOTE ON SYNGE'S LANGUAGE

The authenticity of Synge's peasant dialect was from the first a subject of controversy. It was argued that no Irish man or woman spoke like the characters in his plays. Synge claimed, on the contrary, that in his drama "I have used one or two words only that I have not heard among the country people of Ireland" (*Plays* II, p. 53). It is now fairly generally agreed that the language of the plays was Synge's own poetic creation, although he did use many phrases he had actually heard and grammatical constructions characteristic of the Irish-speaking people of Aran and other parts of Ireland. For detailed discussions of the issue see particularly Alan Bliss, "The Language of Synge," in *J.M. Synge Centenary Papers 1971*, ed. Maurice Harmon, pp. 35-62, Nicholas Grene, *Synge: a Critical Study of the Plays*, pp. 27-29, 60-83, and Declan Kiberd, *Synge and the Irish Language*, pp. 196-215.

The commonest constructions and idioms which differentiate Synge's dialect from standard English are listed below, followed by a brief glossary of the meaning of unusual words and phrases frequently used in the play. Dialect expressions used only once in the text are glossed in the notes.

1. The like of, the way that, what way, the time. *Examples:*
   "a white beautiful skin—*the like of* my skin" = *like* my skin.
   "they'd think it a fine thing if they had us deceived, *the way that* we wouldn't know we were so fine-looking at all" = *so that* we wouldn't know . . .
   "*what way* would I find" = *how* would I find
   "they do have great joy, *the time* they do be seeing a grand thing" = *when* they see . . .

2. Omitted relative pronoun. *Examples:*
   "I do be thinking in the long nights it'd be a grand thing" = I do be thinking . . . *that* it'd be a grand thing.
   "I'm thinking, this time, it's a strange thing surely" = I'm thinking . . . *that* it's a strange thing surely.

3. Continuous forms of the verb.
   In the Anglo-Irish dialect continuous forms of the verb—"I am going" rather than "I go" etc.—are used much more often than in standard English. The habitual form "do be going" is also common. *Examples:*
   "I'm thinking," "they'll be picking it out," "they do be always sitting here."

4. "And" construction. *Examples:*

"it's more I got a while since, *and I sitting* blinded in Grianan" = *when I was sitting . . .*

"What way wouldn't it be cold, *and it freezing since* the moon was changed" = *as it has been freezing*

"how you'd look, *and you* a saint = *if you were* a saint

5. "It's" construction.

In Anglo-Irish, following Irish, any word could be brought forward to the beginning of the sentence for emphasis, prefaced by "it's." This was particularly common in replies to questions. *Examples:*

"*it's little* I know of faces" = I know little of faces

"*it's a* raw beastly day we do have each day" = we have a raw beastly day each day.

"Would we have a right to be crawling in below under the sticks? *It's hard set* I am to know what would be right" = I am hard set

6. "Itself." *Examples:*

"If it's raggy and dirty you are *itself*" = *even if* you are raggy and dirty.

"If you're a liar *itself*" = *even though* you're a liar.

"if it's fine to look on you are *itself*" = *even though* you are . . .

7. "After" construction.

In the Anglo–Irish dialect, "after" + verb generally replaces a perfect tense, particularly where the meaning is "to have just done something." *Examples:*

"*I'm after walking up*" = *I have just walked up*

"a man *is after looking out* a long while on the bad days of the world" = a man *who has looked out . . .*

"Let you not put shame on me *and I after saying* fine words to you" = *when I have said . . .*

GLOSSARY

destroyed
"I'm destroyed this day waiting to look upon her face" = I'm desperate . . .
"and they destroyed with the cold" = terribly cold.

letting on
"letting on she was grand" = pretending she was grand.

lost on
"you have the morning lost on us" = you have made us lose the morning.
"My road is lost on me" = I have lost my road.

a power
"a power of times" = many times
"a power of villainy" = much villainy.

putting . . . on
"putting splendour on a woman" = making a woman splendid.
"putting a fool's head on me" = making a fool of me.
"putting shame on me" = shaming me.

right, rightly
"you'd have a right to step in" = you should step in.
"we don't know rightly" = we don't really know.
"our own blessed water would do rightly" = would do well.

whisht
"Will you whisht, I'm saying?" = Hush.

CRITICAL BIBLIOGRAPHY

This list represents only the more substantial studies of Synge, and the works referred to in this edition. For a comprehensive listing of critical material see: Paul M. Levitt, *J.M. Synge: a Bibliography of Published Criticism* (Dublin: Irish University Press, 1974), E.H. Mikhail, *J.M. Synge: a Bibliography of Criticism* (London: Macmillan, 1975), and Edward A. Kopper, *John Millington Synge: a Reference Guide* (Boston: Hall, 1979).

Bushrui, S.B. (ed.) *Sunshine and the Moon's Delight* (Gerrards Cross, Bucks.: Colin Smythe; Beirut: American University of Beirut, 1972).

Bourgeois, Maurice *John Millington Synge and the Irish Theatre* (London: Constable, 1913; New York: Benjamin Blom, 1965).

Carpenter, Andrew (ed.) *My Uncle John: Edward Stephens's Life of J.M. Synge* (London: Oxford University Press, 1974).

Colum, Padraic *The Road Round Ireland* (New York: Macmillan, 1926).

Corkery, Daniel *Synge and Anglo-Irish Literature* (Dublin & Cork: Cork University Press, 1931; London & New York: Longmans Green, 1931; New York: Russell and Russell, 1965).

Gerstenberger, Donna *John Millington Synge* (New York: Twayne, 1964).

Greene, David H. & Stephens, Edward M. *J.M. Synge 1871-1909* (New York: Macmillan, 1959; Collier Books, 1961).

Gregory, Augusta Lady *Our Irish Theatre* (New York & London: Putnam's, 1913).

Grene, Nicholas *Synge: a Critical Study of the Plays* (London: Macmillan, 1975; Totowa, N.J.: Rowman & Littlefield, 1976).

Harmon, Maurice (ed.) *J.M. Synge Centenary Papers 1971* (Dublin: Dolmen Press, 1972).

Henn, T.R. (ed.) *The Plays and Poems of J.M. Synge* (London: Methuen, 1963).

Hogan, Robert & O'Neill, Michael J. (eds.) *Joseph Holloway's Abbey Theatre* (Carbondale & Edwardsville, Ill.: Southern Illinois University Press; London & Amsterdam: Feffer & Simons, 1967).

Kiberd, Declan *Synge and the Irish Language* (London: Macmillan, 1979).

Mikhail, E.H. (ed.) *J.M. Synge: Interviews and Recollections* (London: Macmillan, 1977).

Price, Alan *Synge and Anglo-Irish Drama* (London: Methuen, 1961).

Saddlemyer, Ann *J.M. Synge and Modern Comedy* (Dublin: Dolmen Press, 1968).

Skelton, Robin *The Writings of J.M. Synge* (London: Thames & Hudson, 1971).

Thornton, Weldon *J.M. Synge and the Western Mind* (Gerrards Cross, Bucks.: Colin Smythe, 1979).

Ulanov, Barry (ed.) *Makers of the Modern Theater* (New York: McGraw Hill, 1961).

Watson, G.J. *Irish Identity and the Literary Revival* (London: Croom Helm, 1979).

Williams, Raymond *Drama from Ibsen to Brecht* (London: Chatto & Windus, 1968).

Worth, Katharine *The Irish Drama of Europe from Yeats to Beckett* (London: Athlone Press, 1978).

THE WELL
OF THE SAINTS

A play in three acts
by
J.M. SYNGE

PERSONS

MARTIN DOUL[1] (a weather-beaten, blind beggar).

MARY DOUL (his wife, a weather-beaten, ugly woman, blind also, nearly fifty).

TIMMY (a middle-aged, almost elderly, but vigorous smith).

MOLLY BYRNE (a fine-looking girl with fair hair).

BRIDE (another handsome girl).

MAT SIMON.

SAINT (a wandering Friar).

OTHER GIRLS AND MEN.

Scene[2]—*Some lonely mountainous district on the east of Ireland one or more centuries ago.*

---

1. DOUL from Ir. "dall" = blind; they are blind Martin and blind Mary, not Mr. and Mrs. Doul.
2. SCENE See Introduction, p. 8.

ACT I.

Scene: *Roadside with big stones, etc., on the right; low loose wall at back with gap near centre; at left, ruined doorway of church with bushes beside it.* MARTIN DOUL *and* MARY DOUL *grope in on left and pass over to stones on right, where they sit.*

MARY DOUL   What place are we now, Martin Doul?

MARTIN DOUL   Passing the gap.

MARY DOUL *[raising her head]*   The length of that! Well, the sun's coming warm this day if it's late autumn itself.

MARTIN DOUL *[putting out his hands in sun]*   What way wouldn't it be warm and it getting high up in the south? You were that length plaiting your yellow hair you have the morning lost on us, and the people are after passing to the fair of Clash.

MARY DOUL   It isn't going to the fair, the time they do be driving their cattle and they with a litter of pigs maybe squealing in their carts, they'd give us a thing at all. *[She sits down.]* It's well you know that, but you must be talking.

MARTIN DOUL *[sitting down beside her and beginning to shred rushes[3] she gives him]*   If I didn't talk I'd be destroyed in a short

---

3. *beginning to shred rushes*   The pith of the shredded rushes would be used to make rush-lights, a type of candle.

while listening to the clack you do be making, for you've a queer cracked voice, the Lord have mercy on you, if it's fine to look on you are itself.

MARY DOUL   Who wouldn't have a cracked voice sitting out all the year in the rain falling? It's a bad life for the voice, Martin Doul, though I've heard tell there isn't anything like the wet south wind does be blowing upon us, for keeping a white beautiful skin—the like of my skin—on your neck and on your brows, and there isn't anything at all like a fine skin for putting splendour on a woman.

MARTIN DOUL *[teasingly, but with good-humour]*   I do be thinking odd times we don't know rightly what way you have your splendour, or asking myself, maybe, if you have it at all, for the time I was a young lad, and had fine sight, it was the ones with sweet voices were the best in face.

MARY DOUL   Let you not be making the like of that talk when you've heard Timmy the smith, and Mat Simon, and Patch Ruadh, and a power besides[4] saying fine things of my face, and you know rightly it was "the beautiful dark woman",[5] they did call me in Ballinatone.[6]

MARTIN DOUL *[as before]*   If it was itself I heard Molly Byrne saying at the fall of night it was little more than a fright you were.

MARY DOUL *[sharply]*   She was jealous, God forgive her, because Timmy the smith was after praising my hair—

MARTIN DOUL *[with mock irony]*   Jealous!

MARY DOUL   Ay, jealous, Martin Doul, and if she wasn't itself, the young and silly do be always making game of them that's dark, and they'd think it a fine thing if they had us deceived, the way we wouldn't know we were so fine-looking at all. *[She puts her hand to her face with a complacent gesture.[7]]*

MARTIN DOUL *[a little plaintively]*   I do be thinking in the long nights it'd be a grand thing if we could see ourselves for one hour, or a minute itself, the way we'd know surely we were the finest man and the finest woman of the seven counties

---

4. *and a power besides* = and many more.

5. *"the beautiful dark woman"*   "Dark" here, and frequently throughout the play, means "blind".

6. *Ballinatone*   The next townland to Grianan where the first act is set.

7. complacent gesture.   *1905 (Quinn)* adds *smooths her hair back with her hands* but the extra phrase is not in *1905*.

of the east . . . *[bitterly]* and then the seeing rabble below[8] might be destroying their souls telling bad lies, and we'd never heed a thing they'd say.

MARY DOUL   If you weren't a big fool you wouldn't heed them this hour Martin Doul, for they're a bad lot those that have their sight, and they do have great joy, the time they do be seeing a grand thing, to let on they don't see it at all, and to be telling fools' lies, the like of what Molly Byrne was telling to yourself.

MARTIN DOUL   If it's lies she does be telling she's a sweet beautiful voice you'd never tire to be hearing, if it was only the pig she'd be calling, or crying out in the long grass, maybe, after her hens. *[Speaking pensively.]* It should be a fine soft, rounded woman, I'm thinking, would have a voice the like of that.

MARY DOUL *[sharply again, scandalized]*   Let you not be minding if it's flat or rounded she is, for she's a flighty, foolish woman you'll hear when you're off a long way, and she making a great noise and laughing at the well.

MARTIN DOUL   Isn't laughing a nice thing the time a woman's young?

MARY DOUL *[bitterly]*   A nice thing is it? A nice thing to hear a woman making a loud braying laugh the like of that? Ah, she's a great one for drawing the men, and you'll hear Timmy himself, the time he does be sitting in his forge, getting mighty fussy if she'll come walking from Grianan, the way you'll hear his breath going, and he wringing his hands.

MARTIN DOUL *[slightly piqued]*   I've heard him say a power of times it's nothing at all she is when you see her at the side of you, and yet I never heard any man's breath getting uneasy the time he'd be looking on yourself.

MARY DOUL   I'm not the like of the girls do be running round on the roads, swinging their legs, and they with their necks out looking on the men. . . . Ah, there's a power of villainy walking the world, Martin Doul, among them that do be gadding around, with their gaping eyes, and their sweet words, and they with no sense in them at all.

MARTIN DOUL *[sadly]*   It's the truth, maybe, and yet I'm told it's a grand thing to see a young girl walking the road.

MARY DOUL   You'd be as bad as the rest of them if you

---

8. *the seeing rabble below*   The villagers who live further down the glen.

had your sight, and I did well surely, not to marry a seeing man—it's scores would have had me and welcome,—for the seeing is a queer lot, and you'd never know the thing they'd do. *[A moment's pause.]*

MARTIN DOUL *[listening]* There's someone coming on the road.

MARY DOUL Let you put the pith[9] away out of their sight, or they'll be picking it out with the spying eyes they have, and saying it's rich we are, and not sparing us a thing at all. *[They bundle away the rushes.* TIMMY *comes in on left.]*

MARTIN DOUL *[with a begging voice]* Leave a bit of silver for blind Martin, your honour. Leave a bit of silver, or a penny copper itself, and we'll be praying the Lord to bless you and you going the way.

TIMMY *[stopping before them]* And you letting on a while back you knew my step! *[He sits down.]*

MARTIN DOUL *[with his natural voice]* I know it when Molly Byrne's walking in front, or when she's two perches,[10] maybe, lagging behind, but it's few times I've heard you walking up the like of that, as if you'd met a thing wasn't right and you coming on the road.

TIMMY *[hot and breathless, wiping his face]* You've good ears, God bless you, if you're a lair itself, for I'm after walking up in great haste from hearing wonders in the fair.

MARTIN DOUL *[rather contemptuously]* You're always hearing queer wonderful things, and the lot of them nothing at all, but I'm thinking, this time, it's a strange thing surely, you'd be walking up before the turn of day, and not waiting below to look on them lepping, or dancing, or playing shows on the green of Clash.

TIMMY *[huffed]* I was coming to tell you it's in this place there'd be a bigger wonder done in a short while *[MARTIN DOUL stops working and looks at him],* than was ever done on the green of Clash, or the width of Leinster itself, but you're thinking, maybe, you're too cute a little fellow to be minding me at all.[11]

---

9. *pith* The pith of the rushes—see n. 3, p. 37.

10. *perches* The perch was a unit of measurement, 5½ yards.

11. *too cute a little fellow to be minding me at all.* = too clever to pay any attention to me. "Cute," from "acute," always means "cunning" or "shrewd" in Ireland.

MARTIN DOUL [*amused but incredulous*] There'll be wonders in this place is it?

TIMMY Here at the crossing of the roads.

MARTIN DOUL I never heard tell of anything to happen in this place since the night they killed the old fellow going home with his gold, the Lord have mercy on him, and threw down his corpse into the bog. Let them not be doing the like of that this night, for it's ourselves have a right to the crossing roads, and we don't want any of your bad tricks, or your wonders either, for it's wonder enough we are ourselves.

TIMMY If I'd a mind I'd be telling you of a real wonder this day, and the way you'll be having a great joy, maybe, you're not thinking on at all.

MARTIN DOUL [*interested*] Are they putting up a still[12] behind in the rocks? It'd be a grand thing if I'd a sup handy the way I wouldn't be destroying myself groping up across the bogs in the rain falling.

TIMMY [*still moodily*] It's not a still they're bringing or the like of it either.

MARY DOUL [*persuasively, to* TIMMY] Maybe they're hanging a thief above at the bit of a tree? I'm told it's a great sight to see a man hanging by his neck, but what joy would that be to ourselves, and we not seeing it at all?

TIMMY [*more pleasantly*] They're hanging no one this day, Mary Doul, and yet with the help of God, you'll see a power hanged before you die.

MARY DOUL Well you've queer humbugging talk. . . . What way would I see a power hanged, and I a dark woman since the seventh year of my age?

TIMMY Did ever you hear tell of a place across a bit of the sea, where there is an island, and the grave of the four beautiful saints?[13]

MARY DOUL I've heard people have walked round from the west and they speaking of that.

TIMMY [*impressively*] There's a green ferny well, I'm told, behind of that place, and if you put a drop of the water

12. *still*—for making poteen (illicit whiskey).

13. *the grave of the four beautiful saints?* The *Teampal Ceathair Aluinn* (the Church of the Four Beauties) is on Aran. Synge records the story of a miraculous cure for blindness effected by the water from the holy well near the church in *The Aran Islands* (*Prose*, pp. 56–7).

out of it on the eyes of a blind man, you'll make him see as well as any person is walking the world.

MARTIN DOUL [*with excitement*] Is that the truth, Timmy? I'm thinking you're telling a lie.

TIMMY [*gruffly*] That's the truth, Martin Doul, and you may believe it now, for you're after believing a power of things weren't as likely at all.

MARY DOUL. Maybe we could send a young lad to bring us the water. I could wash a naggin bottle in the morning, and I'm thinking Patch Ruadh would go for it, if we gave him a good drink, and the bit of money we have hid in the thatch.[14]

TIMMY It'd be no good to be sending a sinful man the like of ourselves, for I'm told the holiness of the water does be getting soiled with the villainy of your heart, the time you'd be carrying it, and you looking round on the girls, maybe, or drinking a small sup at a still.

MARTIN DOUL [*with disappointment*] It'd be a long terrible way to be walking ourselves, and I'm thinking that's a wonder will bring small joy to us at all.

TIMMY [*turning on him impatiently*] What is it you want with your walking? It's as deaf as blind you're growing if you're not after hearing me say it's in this place the wonder would be done.

MARTIN DOUL [*with a flash of anger*] If it is can't you open the big slobbering mouth you have and say what way it'll be done, and not be making blather till the fall of night.

TIMMY [*jumping up*] I'll be going on now [MARY DOUL *rises*], and not wasting time talking civil talk with the like of you.

MARY DOUL [*standing up, disguising her impatience*] Let you come here to me, Timmy, and not be minding him at all. [TIMMY *stops, and she gropes up to him and takes him by the coat.*] You're not huffy with myself, and let you tell me the whole story and don't be fooling me more. . . . Is it yourself has brought us the water?

TIMMY It is not, surely.

MARY DOUL Then tell us your wonder, Timmy. . . . What person'll bring it at all?

---

14. *I could wash . . . thatch.* Cut in the prompt-book. A naggin, or noggin, is a quarter of a pint; Patch Ruadh is Irish for red-haired Pat.

TIMMY *[relenting]* It's a fine holy man will bring it, a saint of the Almighty God.[15]

MARY DOUL *[overawed]* A saint is it?

TIMMY Ay, a fine saint, who's going round through the churches of Ireland, with a long cloak on him, and naked feet, for he's brought a sup of the water slung at his side, and, with the like of him, any little drop is enough to cure the dying, or to make the blind see as clear as the gray hawks do be high up, on a still day, sailing the sky.

MARTIN DOUL *[feeling for his stick]* What place is he, Timmy. I'll be walking to him now.

TIMMY Let you stay quiet, Martin. He's straying around saying prayers at the churches and high crosses, between this place and the hills, and he with a great crowd going behind—for it's fine prayers he does be saying, and fasting with it, till he's as thin as one of the empty rushes you have there on your knee[16]—then he'll be coming after to this place to cure the two of you—we're after telling him the way you are[17]—and to say his prayers in the church.

MARTIN DOUL *[turning suddenly to MARY DOUL]* And we'll be seeing ourselves this day. Oh, glory be to God, is it true surely?

MARY DOUL *[very pleased, to TIMMY]* Maybe I'd have time to walk down and get the big shawl I have below, for I do look my best I've heard them say, when I'm dressed up with that thing on my head.

TIMMY You'd have time surely—

MARTIN DOUL *[listening]* Whisht now . . . I hear people again coming by the stream.

TIMMY *[looking out left, puzzled]* It's the young girls I left walking after the saint. . . . They're coming now *[goes up to entrance]* carrying things in their hands, and they walking as easy as you'd see a child walk, who'd have a dozen eggs hid in her bib.

MARTIN DOUL *[listening]* That's Molly Byrne, I'm thinking. *[MOLLY BYRNE and BRIDE come on left and cross to MARTIN DOUL, carrying water-can, SAINT's bell, and cloak.]*

---

15. *a saint of the Almighty God.* Prompt-book: *a man the like of the saints of God.* See Introduction, p. 12.

16. *at the churches . . . knee* Cut in the prompt-book.

17. *we're after telling him the way you are* Cut in the prompt-book.

MOLLY BYRNE [*volubly*] God bless you, Martin. I've holy water here from the grave of the four saints of the west will have you cured in a short while and seeing like ourselves—

TIMMY [*crosses to* MOLLY, *interrupting her*] He's heard that, God help you. But where at all is the saint, and what way is he after trusting the holy water with the likes of you?

MOLLY BYRNE He was afeard to go a far way with the clouds is coming beyond, so he's gone up now through the thick woods to say a prayer at the crosses of Grianan, and he's coming on this road to the church.

TIMMY [*still astonished*] And he's after leaving the holy water with the two of you? It's a wonder, surely. [*Comes down left a little.*]

MOLLY BYRNE The lads told him no person could carry them things through the briars, and steep, slippy-feeling rocks he'll be climbing above, so he looked round then, and gave the water, and his big cloak, and his bell to the two of us, for young girls, says he, are the cleanest holy people you'd see walking the world. [MARY DOUL *goes near seat.*]

MARY DOUL [*sits down, laughing to herself*] Well, the saint's a simple fellow, and it's no lie.

MARTIN DOUL [*leaning forward, holding out his hands*] Let you give me the water in my hand, Molly Byrne, the way I'll know you have it surely.

MOLLY BYRNE [*giving it to him*] Wonders is queer things, and maybe it'd cure you, and you holding it alone.

MARTIN DOUL [*looking round*] It does not, Molly. I'm not seeing at all. [*He shakes the can.*] There's a small sup only. Well, isn't it a great wonder the little trifling thing would bring seeing to the blind, and be showing us the big women and the young girls, and all the fine things is walking the world. [*He feels for* MARY DOUL *and gives her the can.*]

MARY DOUL [*shaking it*] Well, glory be to God—

MARTIN DOUL [*pointing to* BRIDE] And what is it herself has, making sounds in her hand?

BRIDE [*crossing to* MARTIN DOUL] It's the saint's bell, you'll hear him ringing out the time he'll be going up some place, to be saying his prayers. [MARTIN DOUL *holds out his hands; she gives it to him.*]

MARTIN DOUL [*ringing it*] It's a sweet, beautiful sound.

MARY DOUL   You'd know I'm thinking by the little silvery voice of it, a fasting holy man was after carrying it a great way at his side. [BRIDE *crosses a little right behind* MARTIN DOUL.]

MOLLY BYRNE [*unfolding* SAINT's *cloak*]   Let you stand up now, Martin Doul, till I put his big cloak on you the way[18] we'd see how you'd look, and you a saint of the Almighty God.

MARTIN DOUL [*standing up, a little diffidently*]   I've heard the priests a power of times, making great talk and praises of the beauty of the saints. [MOLLY BYRNE *slips cloak round him.*]

TIMMY [*uneasily*]   You'd have a right to be leaving him alone, Molly. What would the saint say if he seen you making game with his cloak?

MOLLY BYRNE [*recklessly*]   How would he see us, and he saying prayers in the wood? [*She turns* MARTIN DOUL *round.*]   Isn't that a fine holy-looking saint, Timmy the smith? [*Laughing foolishly.*]   There's a grand handsome fellow, Mary Doul, and if you seen him now, you'd be as proud, I'm thinking, as the archangels below, fell out with the Almighty God.[19]

MARY DOUL [*with quiet confidence going to* MARTIN DOUL *and feeling his cloak*]   It's proud we'll be this day surely. [MARTIN DOUL *is still ringing.*]

MOLLY BYRNE [*to* MARTIN DOUL]   Would you think well to be all your life walking round the like of that Martin Doul, and you bell-ringing with the saints of God?

MARY DOUL [*turning on her, fiercely*]   How would he be bell-ringing with the saints of God and he wedded with myself?

MARTIN DOUL   It's the truth she's saying, and if bell-ringing is a fine life, yet I'm thinking, maybe, it's better I am wedded with the beautiful dark woman of Ballinatone.

MOLLY BYRNE [*scornfully*]   You're thinking that, God help you, but it's little you know of her at all.

---

18. *on you the way*   1905: *on you.* [MARTIN DOUL rises, comes forward, centre a little.] *The way*   The 1905 stage direction, which is not in the prompt-book, is incompatible with Martin's next speech which gives him *standing up, a little diffidently*.

19. *the archangels below, fell out with the Almighty God.*   Synge explained this as "the archangels down in hell that quarrelled or fought with the A. God" (*Plays* I, p. 84).

MARTIN DOUL   It's little surely, and I'm destroyed this day waiting to look upon her face.

TIMMY *[awkwardly]*   It's well you know the way she is, for the like of you do have great knowledge in the feeling of your hands.

MARTIN DOUL *[still feeling the cloak]*   We do maybe. . . . Yet it's little I know of faces, or of fine beautiful cloaks, for it's few cloaks I've had my hand to, and few faces, *[plaintively]* for the young girls is mighty shy, Timmy the smith, and it isn't much they heed me, though they do be saying I'm a handsome man.

MARY DOUL *[mockingly, with good-humour]*   Isn't it a queer thing the voice he puts on him, when you hear him talking of the skinny young-looking girls, and he married with a woman he's heard called the wonder of the western world?

TIMMY *[pityingly]*   The two of you will see a great wonder this day, and it's no lie.

MARTIN DOUL   I've heard tell her yellow hair, and her white skin, and her big eyes are a wonder, surely—

BRIDE *[who has looked out left]*   Here's the saint coming from the selvage[20] of the wood. . . . Strip the cloak from him, Molly, or he'll be seeing it now.

MOLLY BYRNE *[hastily to BRIDE]*   Take the bell and put herself by the stones. *[To MARTIN DOUL.]* Will you hold your head up till I loosen the cloak. *[She pulls off the cloak and throws it over her arm. Then she pushes MARTIN DOUL over and stands him beside MARY DOUL.]* Stand there now, quiet, and let you not be saying a word. *[She and BRIDE stand a little on their left, demurely, with bell, etc., in their hands.]*

MARTIN DOUL *[nervously arranging his clothes]*   Will he mind the way we are, and we not tidied or washed cleanly at all?

MOLLY BYRNE   He'll not see what way you are. . . . He'd walk by the finest woman in Ireland, I'm thinking, and not trouble to raise his two eyes to look upon her face. . . . Whisht! *[SAINT comes on left, with crowd.]*

SAINT   Are these the two poor people?

TIMMY *[officiously]*   They are, holy father, they do be always sitting here at the crossing of the roads, asking a bit of copper[21] from them that do pass, or stripping rushes for lights,

---

20. *selvage* = edge, originally of cloth.

21. *a bit of copper* = money, small change.

and they not mournful at all, but talking out straight with a full voice, and making game with them that likes it.

SAINT [to MARTIN DOUL *and* MARY DOUL] It's a hard life you've had not seeing sun or moon, or the holy priests itself praying to the Lord, but it's the like of you who are brave in a bad time will make a fine use of the gift of sight the Almighty God will bring to you to-day. [*He takes his cloak and puts it about him.*] It's on a bare starving rock[22] that there's the grave of the four beauties of God, the way it's little wonder, I'm thinking, if it's with bare starving people the water should be used. [*He takes the water and bell and slings them round his shoulders.*] So it's to the like of yourselves I do be going, who are wrinkled and poor, a thing rich men would hardly look at at all, but would throw a coin to, or a crust of bread.

MARTIN DOUL [*moving uneasily*] When they look on herself who is a fine woman—

TIMMY [*shaking him*] Whisht now, and be listening to the saint.

SAINT [*looks at them a moment, continues*] If it's raggy and dirty you are itself, I'm saying, the Almighty God isn't at all like the rich men of Ireland, and with the power of the water I'm after bringing in a little curragh into Cashla Bay,[23] He'll have pity on you, and put sight into your eyes.

MARTIN DOUL [*taking off his hat*] I'm ready now, holy father—

SAINT [*taking him by the hand*] I'll cure you first, and then I'll come for your wife. We'll go up now into the church, for I must say a prayer to the Lord. [*To* MARY DOUL, *as he moves off.*][24] And let you be making your mind still and saying praises in your heart, for it's a great wonderful thing when the power of the Lord of the world is brought down upon your like.

PEOPLE [*pressing after him*] Come now till we watch.

BRIDE Come, Timmy.

SAINT [*waving them back*] Stay back where you are, for I'm not wanting a big crowd making whispers in the church. Stay back there, I'm saying, and you'd do well to be thinking

---

22. *bare starving rock* = Aran. See n. 13, p. 41.

23. *curragh into Cashla Bay* The curragh is a light canoe; Cashla Bay is an inlet on the coast of Galway.

24. *We'll go . . . moves off.*] Cut in the prompt-book.

on the way sin has brought blindness to the world, and to be
saying a prayer for your own sakes against false prophets and
heathens, and the words of women and smiths, and all knowledge that would soil the soul or the body of a man.[25] *[PEOPLE
shrink back. He goes into church. MARY DOUL groping half way
towards the door and kneels near path. PEOPLE form a group at
right.]*

TIMMY   Isn't it a fine, beautiful voice he has, and he a
fine, brave[26] man if it wasn't for the fasting?

BRIDE   Did you watch him moving his hands?

MOLLY BYRNE   It'd be a fine thing if some one in this
place could pray the like of him, for I'm thinking the water
from our own blessed well would do rightly if a man knew the
way to be saying prayers, and then there'd be no call to be
bringing water from that wild place, where, I'm told, there are
no decent houses, or fine-looking people at all.

BRIDE *[who is looking in at door from right]*   Look at the
great trembling Martin has, shaking him, and he on his knees.

TIMMY *[anxiously]*   God help him. . . . What will he be
doing when he sees his wife this day? I'm thinking it was bad
work we did when we let on she was fine-looking, and not a
wrinkled wizened hag the way she is.

MAT SIMON   Why would he be vexed, and we after
giving him great joy and pride, the time he was dark?

MOLLY BYRNE *[sitting down in MARY DOUL's seat and
tidying her hair]*   If it's vexed he is itself, he'll have other things
now to think on as well as his wife, and what does any man
care for a wife, when it's two weeks, or three, he is looking on
her face?

MAT SIMON   That's the truth now, Molly, and it's more
joy dark Martin got from the lies we told of that hag is kneel-
ing by the path, than your own man will get from you, day or
night, and he living at your side.

MOLLY BYRNE *[defiantly]*   Let you not be talking, Mat
Simon, for it's not yourself will be my man, though you'd be

---

25. *a prayer . . . body of a man.*   Closely based on the ancient Irish hymn,
"St. Patrick's Breastplate". "In Irish folklore," according to Synge, "smiths
were thought to be magicians, and more or less in league with the powers of
darkness" (*Plays* I, p. 90).

26. *brave*   A general term of physical praise, like the Scots "braw," rather
than "courageous."

crowing and singing fine songs if you'd that hope in you at all.

TIMMY [*shocked, to* MOLLY BYRNE] Let you not be raising your voice when the saint's above at his prayers.

BRIDE [*crying out*] Whisht. . . . Whisht. . . . I'm thinking he's cured.

MARTIN DOUL [*crying out in the church*] Oh, glory be to God—

SAINT [*solemnly*] Laus patri sit et filio cum spiritu paraclito

Qui suae dono gratiae misertus est Hiberniae—[27]

MARTIN DOUL [*ecstatically*] Oh, glory be to God, I see now surely. . . . I see the walls of the church, and yourself,[28] holy father, and the great width of the sky. [*He runs out half foolish with joy, and comes past* MARY DOUL *as she scrambles to her feet, drawing a little away from her as he goes by.*]

TIMMY [*to the others*] He doesn't know her at all. [SAINT *comes out behind* MARTIN DOUL *and leads* MARY DOUL *into the church.* MARTIN DOUL *comes on to* PEOPLE. *The Men are between him and the Girls, he verifies his position with his stick.*]

MARTIN DOUL [*crying out joyfully*] That's Timmy, I know Timmy by the black of his head. . . . That's Mat Simon, I know Mat by the length of his legs. . . . That should be Patch Ruadh, with the gamey eyes[29] in him, and the fiery hair. [*He sees* MOLLY BYRNE *on* MARY DOUL's *seat, and his voice changes completely.*] Oh, it was no lie they told me, Mary Doul. Oh, glory to God and the seven saints I didn't die and not see you at all.[30] The blessing of God on the water, and the feet carried it round through the land, for it's grand hair[31] you have [*she lowers her head a little confused*], and soft skin, and eyes would

---

27. *Oh glory . . . Hiberniae* Cut in the prompt-book. This cut was made because W.G. Fay, the play's director, thought that the climax was retarded, but Synge himself did not think it necessary (*Plays* I, p. 92). The Saint's Latin prayer means "Praise be to the Father and to the Son with the Holy Spirit, Who by His gift of grace took pity on Ireland."

28. *church, and yourself* 1905: *church, and the green bits of ferns in them, and yourself.*

29. *gamey eyes* = "tricky, merry eyes"—Synge's gloss (*Plays* I, p. 94).

30. *and not see you at all.* Prompt-book adds stage direction here: (*All turn back and look at Martin and Molly*).

31. *land, for it's grand* 1905: *land. The blessing of God on this day, and them that brought me the Saint, for it's grand*

make the saints, if they were dark awhile and seeing again, fall down out of the sky. *[He goes nearer to her.]* Hold up your head, Mary, the way I'll see it's richer I am than the great kings of the east. Hold up your head, I'm saying, for it's soon you'll be seeing me, and I not a bad one at all. *[He touches her and she starts up.]*

MOLLY BYRNE   Let you keep away from me, and not be soiling my chin. *[PEOPLE laugh loudly.]*

MARTIN DOUL *[bewildered]*   It's Molly's voice you have.

MOLLY BYRNE   Why wouldn't I have my own voice? Do you think I'm a ghost?

MARTIN DOUL   Which of you all is herself? *[He goes up to BRIDE.]* Is it you is Mary Doul? I'm thinking you're more the like of what they said. *[Peering at her.]* For you've yellow hair, and white skin, and it's the smell of my own turf is rising from your shawl. *[He catches her shawl.]*

BRIDE *[pulling away her shawl]*   I'm not your wife, and let you get out of my way. *[PEOPLE laugh again.]*

MARTIN DOUL *[with misgiving, to another Girl]*   Is it yourself it is? You're not so fine looking, but I'm thinking you'd do, with the grand nose you have, and your nice hands and your feet.

GIRL *[scornfully]*   I never seen any person that took me for blind, and a seeing woman, I'm thinking, would never wed the like of you. *[She turns away, and PEOPLE laugh once more, drawing back a little and leaving him on their left.]*

PEOPLE *[jeeringly]*   Try again, Martin, try again, you'll find her yet.[32]

MARTIN DOUL *[passionately]*   Where is it you have her hidden away? Isn't it a black shame for a drove of pitiful beasts the like of you to be making game of me, and putting a fool's head on me the grand day of my life? Ah, you're thinking you're a fine lot, with your giggling, weeping eyes, a fine lot to be making game of myself, and the woman I've heard called the great wonder of the west. . . . *[During this speech, which he gives with his back towards the church, MARY DOUL has come out with her sight cured, and come down towards the right with a silly simpering smile, till she is a little behind MARTIN DOUL.]*

MARY DOUL *[when he pauses]*   Which of you is Martin Doul?

_____

32. *try again, you'll find her yet.   1905: try again, and you'll be finding her yet.*

MARTIN DOUL *[wheeling round]* It's her voice surely. *[They stare at each other blankly.]*

MOLLY BYRNE *[to MARTIN DOUL]* Go up now and take her under the chin and be speaking the way you spoke to myself.

MARTIN DOUL *[in a low voice, with intensity]* If I speak now, I'll speak hard to the two of you—33

MOLLY BYRNE *[to MARY DOUL]* You're not saying a word, Mary. What is it you think of himself, with the fat legs on him, and the little neck like a ram?

MARY DOUL I'm thinking it's a poor thing when the Lord God gives you sight, and puts the like of that man in your way.

MARTIN DOUL It's on your two knees you should be thanking the Lord God you're not looking on yourself, for if it was yourself you seen, you'd be running round in a short while like the old screeching madwoman is running round in the glen.

MARY DOUL *[beginning to realize herself]* If I'm not so fine as some of them said, I have my hair, and my big eyes,34 and my white skin—

MARTIN DOUL *[breaking out into a passionate cry]* Your hair, and your big eyes is it? . . . I'm telling you there isn't a wisp on any gray mare on the ridge of the world isn't finer than the dirty twist on your head. There isn't two eyes in any starving sow, isn't finer than the eyes you were calling blue like the sea.

MARY DOUL *[interrupting him]* It's the devil cured you this day, and drove35 you crazy with lies.

MARTIN DOUL Isn't it yourself is after playing lies on me, ten years, in the day and in the night, but what is that to you now36 the Lord God has given eyes to me, the way I see you an old, wizendy hag, was never fit to rear a child to me itself.

MARY DOUL I wouldn't rear a crumpled whelp the like

---

33. *I'll speak hard to the two of you—* Presumably addressed to Molly Byrne and Timmy.

34. *my hair, and my big eyes.* 1905: *my hair, and big eyes.*

35. *day, and drove* 1905: *day with your talking of sows; it's the devil cured you this day, I'm saying, and drove*

36. *what is that to you now* = what good is that to you now.

of you. It's many a woman is married with finer than yourself should be praising God if she's no child, and isn't loading the earth with things would make the heavens lonesome above, and they scaring the angels[37] passing in the sky.

MARTIN DOUL   Go on now to be seeking a lonesome place where the earth can hide you away, go on now, I'm saying, or you'll be having men and women with their knees bled, and they screaming to God for a holy water would darken their sight, for there's no man but would liefer[38] be blind a hundred years, or a thousand itself, than to be looking on your like.

MARY DOUL *[raising her stick]*   Maybe if I hit you a strong blow you'd be blind again, and having what you want— *[SAINT is seen in church-door with his head bent in prayer.]*

MARTIN DOUL *[raising his stick and driving MARY DOUL back towards left]*   Let you keep off from me now if you wouldn't have me strike out the little handful of brains you have about on the road. *[He is going to strike her, but TIMMY catches him by the arm.]*

TIMMY   Have you no shame to be making a great row and the saint above saying his prayers?

MARTIN DOUL   What is it I care for the like of him? *[Struggling to free himself.]* Let me hit her one good one for the love of the Almighty God, and I'll be quiet after till I die.

TIMMY *[shaking him]*   Will you whisht, I'm saying.

SAINT *[coming forward, centre]*   Are their minds troubled with joy, or is their sight uncertain the way it does often be the day a person is restored?

TIMMY   It's too certain their sight is, holy father, and they're after making a great fight, because they're a pair of pitiful shows.

SAINT *[coming between them]*   May the Lord who has given you sight send a little sense into your heads, the way it won't be on your two selves you'll be looking—on two pitiful sinners of the earth—but on the splendour of the Spirit of God, you'll see an odd time shining out through the big hills, and steep streams falling to the sea. For if it's on the like of that you do be thinking, you'll not be minding the faces of men,

---

37. *scaring the angels   1905: scaring the larks, and the crows, and the angels*
38. *liefer* = rather.

but you'll be saying prayers and great praises, till you'll be living the way the great saints do be living, with little but old sacks, and skin covering their bones. *[To* TIMMY.*]* Leave him go now, you're seeing he's quiet again. *[*TIMMY *frees* MARTIN DOUL.*]* And let you *[*SAINT *turns to* MARY DOUL*]* not be raising your voice, a bad thing in a woman, but let the lot of you, who have seen the power of the Lord, be thinking on it in the dark night, and be saying to yourselves it's great pity, and love He has, for the poor, starving people of Ireland. *[He gathers his cloak about him.]* And now the Lord send blessing to you all, for I am going on to Annagolan, where there is a deaf woman, and to Laragh where there are two men without sense, and to Glenassil where there are children, blind from their birth, and then I'm going to sleep this night in the bed of the holy Kevin,[39] and to be praising God, and asking great blessing on you all. *[He bends his head.]*

CURTAIN.

---

39. *the bed of the holy Kevin,* "St. Kevin's bed" is a stone cell on a cliff beside the upper lake in Glendalough, the place of retreat of the seventh century St. Kevin who founded the monastery of Glendalough.

ACT II.

Scene: *Village roadside; on left the door of a forge, with broken wheels, etc., lying about. A well near centre, with board above it, and room to pass behind it.* MARTIN DOUL *is sitting near forge, cutting sticks.*

TIMMY *[heard hammering inside forge, then calls]* Let you make haste out there. . . . I'll be putting up new fires at the turn of day, and you haven't the half of them cut yet.

MARTIN DOUL *[gloomily]* It's destroyed I'll be whacking your old thorns[40] till the turn of day, and I with no food in my stomach would keep the life in a pig. *[He turns towards the door.]* Let you come out here and cut them yourself if you want them cut, for there's an hour every day when a man has a right to his rest.

TIMMY *[coming out, with a hammer, impatiently]* Do you want me to be driving you off again to be walking the roads? There you are now, and I giving you your food, and a corner to sleep, and money with it, and to hear the talk of you, you'd think I was after beating you, or stealing your gold.

---

40. *whacking your old thorns* Blackthorn is commonly used for firewood in the Irish countryside.

MARTIN DOUL   You'd do it handy maybe,[41] if I'd gold to steal.

TIMMY [throws down hammer; picks up some of the sticks already cut, and throws them into door]   There's no fear of your having gold, a lazy, basking fool the like of you.

MARTIN DOUL   No fear, maybe, and I here with yourself, for it's more I got a while since, and I sitting blinded in Grianan, than I get in this place, working hard, and destroying myself, the length of the day.

TIMMY [stopping with amazement]   Working hard? [He goes over to him.] I'll teach you to work hard, Martin Doul. Strip off your coat now, and put a tuck in your sleeves, and cut the lot of them, while I'd rake the ashes from the forge, or I'll not put up with you another hour itself.

MARTIN DOUL [horrified]   Would you have me getting my death sitting out in the black wintery air with no coat on me at all?

TIMMY [with authority]   Strip if off now, or walk down upon the road.

MARTIN DOUL [bitterly]   Oh, God help me! [He begins taking off his coat.] I've heard tell you stripped the sheet from your wife and you putting her down into the grave, and that there isn't the like of you for plucking your living ducks,[42] the short days, and leaving them running round in their skins, in the great rains and the cold. [He tucks up his sleeves.] Ah, I've heard a power of queer things of yourself, and there isn't one of them I'll not believe from this day, and be telling to the boys.

TIMMY [pulling over a big stick]   Let you cut that now, and give me rest from your talk, for I'm not heeding you at all.

MARTIN DOUL [taking stick]   That's a hard terrible stick,[43] Timmy, and isn't it a poor thing to be cutting strong timber the like of that, when it's cold the bark is, and slippy with the frost of the air?

TIMMY [gathering up another armful of sticks]   What way wouldn't it be cold, and it freezing since the moon was

---

41. You'd do it handy, maybe, = you might easily do it.

42. plucking your living ducks,   On Aran Synge had observed women "plucking the feathers from live ducks and geese" (Prose, p. 163).

43. hard terrible stick,   "Stick" is used in Ireland for wood of various sizes from a twig up to a fairly large log.

changed? *[He goes into forge.]*

MARTIN DOUL *[querulously, as he cuts slowly]* What way, indeed, Timmy? For it's a raw, beastly day we do have each day, till I do be thinking it's well for the blind, don't be seeing them gray clouds driving on the hill, and don't be looking on people with their noses red, the like of your nose, and their eyes weeping, and watering, the like of your eyes, God help you, Timmy the smith.

TIMMY *[seen blinking in doorway]* Is it turning now you are against your sight?

MARTIN DOUL *[very miserably]* It's a hard thing for a man to have his sight, and he living near to the like of you, *[he cuts a stick, and throws it away]* or wed with a wife, *[cuts a stick]* and I do be thinking it should be a hard thing for the Almighty God to be looking on the world, bad days, and on men the like of yourself walking around on it, and they slipping each way in the muck.

TIMMY *[with pot-hooks which he taps on anvil]* You'd have a right to be minding, Martin Doul, for it's a power the saint cured lose their sight after a while—it's well you know Mary Doul's dimming again—and I'm thinking[44] the Lord if He hears you making that talk will have little pity left for you at all.

MARTIN DOUL There's not a bit of fear of me losing my sight, and if it's a dark day itself it's too well I see every wicked wrinkle you have round by your eye.

TIMMY *[looking at him sharply]* Dark day is it?[45] The day's not dark since the clouds broke in the east.

MARTIN DOUL Let you not be tormenting yourself trying to make me afeard. You told me a power of bad lies the time I was blind, and it's right now for you to stop, and be taking your rest *[MARY DOUL comes in unnoticed on right with a sack filled with green stuff on her arm]*, for it's little ease or quiet any person would get if the big fools of Ireland weren't weary at times. *[He looks up and sees MARY DOUL.]* Oh, glory be to God, she's coming again. *[He begins to work busily with his back to her.]*

---

44. *after a while . . . and I'm thinking* 1905: *after a while. Mary Doul's dimming again I've heard them say—and I'm thinking*

45. *Dark day is it?* This phrase was added to *1905* "to emphasize the situation" in the theatre (*Plays* I, p. 106).

TIMMY [amused, to MARY DOUL, as she is going by without looking at them] Look on him now, Mary Doul. You'd be a great one for keeping him steady at his work, for he's after idling, and blathering, to this hour from the dawn of day.

MARY DOUL [stiffly] Of what is it you're speaking, Timmy the smith?

TIMMY [laughing] Of himself, surely. Look on him there, and he with the shirt on him ripping from his back. You'd have a right to come round this night, I'm thinking, and put a stitch into his clothes, for it's long enough you are, not speaking one to the other.

MARY DOUL Let the two of you not torment me at all. [She goes out left, with her head in the air.]

MARTIN DOUL [stops work and looks after her] Well, isn't it a queer thing she can't keep herself two days without looking on my face?

TIMMY [jeeringly] Looking on your face is it? And she after going by with her head turned the way you'd see a priest going where there'd be a drunken man in the side ditch talking with a girl.[46] [MARTIN DOUL gets up and goes to corner of forge, and looks out left.]

TIMMY Come back here and don't mind her at all. Come back here, I'm saying, you've no call to be spying behind her since she went off, and left you, in place of breaking her heart, trying to keep you in the decency of clothes and food.

MARTIN DOUL [crying out indignantly] You know rightly, Timmy, it was myself drove her away.

TIMMY That's a lie you're telling, yet it's little I care which one of you was driving the other, and let you walk back here I'm saying to your work.

MARTIN DOUL [turning round] I'm coming surely. [He stops and looks out right, going a step or two towards centre.][47]

TIMMY On what is it you're gaping, Martin Doul?

MARTIN DOUL There'a a person walking above. . . . It's Molly Byrne I'm thinking, coming down with her can.

---

46. the way . . . girl. Prompt-book and 1905 (JMS): the way you'd see a sainted lady going where there'd be drunken people in the side ditch singing to themselves. See Note on the Text, p. 29.

47. [He stops . . . centre.] Cut in the prompt-book along with Timmy's speech following.

TIMMY   If she is itself let you not be idling this day, or minding her at all, and let you hurry with them sticks, for I'll want you in a short while to be blowing in the forge. *[He throws down pot-hooks.]*

MARTIN DOUL *[crying out]*   Is it roasting me now, you'd be? *[Turns back and sees pot-hooks, he takes them up.]* Pot-hooks?[48] Is it over them you've been inside sneezing and sweating since the dawn of day?

TIMMY *[resting himself on anvil, with satisfaction]*   I'm making a power of things you do have when you're settling with a wife, Martin Doul, for I heard tell last night the saint'll be passing again in a short while, and I'd have him wed Molly with myself. . . . He'd do it, I've heard them say, for not a penny at all.[49]

MARTIN DOUL *[lays down hooks and looks at him steadily]*   Molly'll be saying great praises now to the Almighty God and He giving her a fine stout hardy man the like of you.

TIMMY *[uneasily]*   And why wouldn't she, if she's a fine woman itself?

MARTIN DOUL *[looking up right]*   Why wouldn't she indeed, Timmy? . . . The Almighty God's made a fine match in the two of you, for if you went marrying a woman was the like of yourself you'd be having the fearfullest little children, I'm thinking, was ever seen in the world.

TIMMY *[seriously offended]*   God forgive you, if you're an ugly man to be looking at, I'm thinking your tongue's worse than your view.

MARTIN DOUL *[hurt also]*   Isn't it destroyed with the cold I am, and if I'm ugly itself I never seen any one the like of you for dreepiness this day, Timmy the smith, and I'm thinking now herself's coming above you'd have a right to step up into your old shanty, and give a rub to your face, and not be sitting there with your bleary eyes, and your big nose, the like of an old scarecrow stuck down upon the road.

TIMMY *[looking up the road uneasily]*   She's no call to mind what way I look, and I after building a house with four rooms in it above on the hill. *[He stands up.]* But it's a queer thing the

---

48. *Pot-hooks?*   Iron hangers for suspending pots or kettles over an open fire.

49. *He'd do it, I've heard them say, for not a penny at all.*   There would normally be a marriage fee.

way yourself and Mary Doul are after setting every person in this place, and up beyond to Rathvanna,[50] talking of nothing, and thinking of nothing, but the way they do be looking in the face. *[Going towards forge.]* It's the devil's work you're after doing with your talk of fine looks, and I'd do right, maybe, to step in, and wash the blackness from my eyes. *[He goes into forge.* MARTIN DOUL *rubs his face furtively with the tail of his coat.* MOLLY BYRNE *comes on right with a water-can, and begins to fill it at the well.]*

MARTIN DOUL   God save you, Molly Byrne.

MOLLY BYRNE *[indifferently]*   God save you.

MARTIN DOUL   That's a dark, gloomy day, and the Lord have mercy on us all.

MOLLY BYRNE   Middling dark.

MARTIN DOUL   It's a power of dirty days, and dark mornings, and shabby-looking fellows *[he makes a gesture over his shoulder]* we do have to be looking on when we have our sight, God help us, but there's[51] one fine thing we have, to be looking on a grand, white, handsome girl, the like of you . . . and every time I set my eyes on you I do be blessing the saints, and the holy water, and the power of the Lord Almighty in the heavens above.

MOLLY BYRNE   I've heard the priests say it isn't looking on a young girl would teach many to be saying their prayers. *[Baling water into her can with a cup.]*

MARTIN DOUL   It isn't many have been the way I was, hearing your voice speaking, and not seeing you at all.

MOLLY BYRNE   That should have been a queer time for an old wicked, coaxing fool to be sitting there with your eyes shut, and not seeing a sight of girl or woman passing the road.

MARTIN DOUL   If it was a queer time itself, it was great joy and pride I had, the time I'd hear your voice speaking and you passing to Grianan *[beginning to speak with plaintive intensity]*, for it's of many a fine thing your voice would put a poor dark fellow in mind, and the day I'd hear it, it's of little else at all I would be thinking.

MOLLY BYRNE   I'll tell your wife if you talk to me the like of that. . . . You've heard, maybe, she's below picking

50. *Rathvanna,* See Introduction, p. 8.

51. *we do have to be looking on . . . but there's* The prompt-book is altered to read *we do be looking on when we have our sight, but there's*

59

nettles for the widow O'Flinn, who took great pity on her when she seen the two of you fighting, and yourself putting shame on her at the crossing of the roads.

MARTIN DOUL *[impatiently]* Is there no living person can speak a score of words to me, or say "God speed you", itself, without putting me in mind of the old woman, or that day either at Grianan?

MOLLY BYRNE *[maliciously]* I was thinking it should be a fine thing to put you in mind of the day you called the grand day of your life.

MARTIN DOUL Grand day, is it? *[Plaintively again, throwing aside his work, and leaning towards her.]* Or a bad black day when I was roused up and found I was the like of the little children do be listening to the stories of an old woman, and do be dreaming after in the dark night that it's in grand houses of gold they are, with speckled horses to ride, and do be waking again, in a short while, and they destroyed with the cold, and the thatch dripping, maybe, and the starved ass braying in the yard?

MOLLY BYRNE *[working indifferently]* You've great romancing this day, Martin Doul. Was it up at the still[52] you were at the fall of night?

MARTIN DOUL *[stands up, comes toward her, but stands at far (right) side of well]* It was not, Molly Byrne, but lying down in a little rickety shed. . . . Lying down across a sop of straw, and I thinking I was seeing you walk, and hearing the sound of your step on a dry road, and hearing you again, and you laughing and making great talk in a high room with dry timber lining the roof. For it's a fine sound your voice has that time, and it's better I am, I'm thinking, lying down, the way a blind man does be lying, than to be sitting here in the gray light, taking hard words of Timmy the smith.

MOLLY BYRNE *[looking at him with interest]* It's queer talk you have if it's a little, old, shabby stump of a man you are itself.

MARTIN DOUL I'm not so old as you do hear them say.

MOLLY BYRNE You're old, I'm thinking, to be talking that talk with a girl.

MARTIN DOUL *[despondingly]* It's not a lie you're telling maybe, for it's long years I'm after losing from the world,

---

52. *still* See n. 12, p 41.

feeling love, and talking love, with the old woman, and I fooled the whole while with the lies of Timmy the smith.

MOLLY BYRNE [half invitingly] It's a fine way you're wanting to pay Timmy the smith. . . . And it's not his *lies* you're making love to this day, Martin Doul.

MARTIN DOUL It is not, Molly, [he passes behind her and comes near her left], but with the good looks of yourself, for if it's old I am, maybe, I've heard tell[53] there are lands beyond in Cahir Iveraghig and the Reeks of Cork[54] with warm sun in them, and fine light in the sky. [Bending towards her.] And light's a grand thing for a man ever was blind, or a woman, with a fine neck, and a skin on her the like of you, the way we'd have a right to go off this day till we'd have a fine life passing abroad through them towns of the south, and we telling stories, maybe, or singing songs at the fairs.

MOLLY BYRNE [turning round half amused, and looking him over from head to foot] Well, isn't it a queer thing when your own wife's after leaving you because you're a pitiful show, you'd talk the like of that to me?

MARTIN DOUL [drawing back a little, hurt, but indignant] It's a queer thing, maybe, for all things is queer in the world. [In a low voice with peculiar emphasis.] But there's one thing I'm telling you, if she walked off away from me, it wasn't because of seeing me, and I no more than I am, but because I was looking on her with my two eyes, and she getting up, and eating her food, and combing her hair, and lying down for her sleep.

MOLLY BYRNE [interested, off her guard] Wouldn't any married man you'd have be doing the like of that?

MARTIN DOUL [seizing the moment that he has her attention] I'm thinking by the mercy of God it's few sees anything but them is blind for a space. [With excitement.] It's few sees the old women rotting for the grave, and it's few sees the like of yourself— [he bends over her] —though it's shining you are, like a high lamp, would drag in the ships out of the sea.

---

53. *It is not, Molly, . . . I've heard tell*   1905: *It is not, Molly, and the Lord forgive us all.* [He passes behind her and comes near her left.] *For I've heard tell*

54. *Cahir Iveraghig and the Reeks of Cork*   A town and mountains in Kerry, more commonly known as Cahirciveen and the McGillicuddy Reeks. Cahir Iveraghig, the city of Iveragh, is pronounced kắhĭr eevráu-ig, according to Synge (*Plays* I, p. 275).

MOLLY BYRNE [*shrinking away from him*]   Keep off from me, Martin Doul.

MARTIN DOUL [*quickly, with low, furious intensity. He puts his hand on her shoulder and shakes her*]   You'd do right, I'm saying, not to marry[55] a man is after looking out a long while on the bad days of the world, for what way would the like of him have fit eyes to look on yourself, when you rise up in the morning and come out of the little door you have above in the lane, the time it'd be a fine thing if a man would be seeing, and losing his sight, the way he'd have your two eyes facing him, and he going the roads, and shining above him, and he looking in the sky, and springing up from the earth, the time he'd lower his head, in place of the muck that seeing men do meet all roads spread on the world.

MOLLY BYRNE [*who has listened half mesmerized, starting away*]   It's the like of that talk you'd hear from a man would be losing his mind.

MARTIN DOUL [*going after her, passing to her right*]   It'd be little wonder if a man near the like of you would be losing his mind. Put down your can now, and come along with myself, for I'm seeing you this day, seeing you, maybe, the way no man has seen you in the world. [*He takes her by the arm and tries to pull her away softly to the right.*] Let you come on now, I'm saying, to the lands of Iveragh and the Reeks of Cork, where you won't set down the width of your two feet and not be crushing fine flowers, and making sweet smells in the air.

MOLLY BYRNE [*laying down can; trying to free herself*]   Leave me go, Martin Doul! Leave me go, I'm saying!

MARTIN DOUL   Come along now, let you come on the little path[56] through the trees.

MOLLY BYRNE [*crying out towards forge*]   Timmy . . . Timmy the smith . . . [*TIMMY comes out of forge, and MARTIN DOUL lets her go. MOLLY BYRNE, excited and breathless, pointing to MARTIN DOUL.*] Did ever you hear that them that loses their sight loses their sense along with it, Timmy the smith?

TIMMY [*suspicious, but uncertain*]   He's no sense surely,

---

55. [quickly, . . . marry   1905: [Quickly with low, furious intensity.] *It's the truth I'm telling you.* [He puts his hand on her shoulder and shakes her.] *And you'd do right not to marry*

56. MARTIN DOUL. *Come along . . . path*   1905: Martin Doul. *Let you not be fooling. Come along now the little path*

and he'll be having himself driven off this day from where he's good sleeping, and feeding, and wages for his work.

MOLLY BYRNE [as before] He's a bigger fool than that, Timmy. Look on him now, and tell me if that isn't a grand fellow to think he's only to open his mouth to have a fine woman, the like of me, running along by his heels. [MARTIN DOUL recoils towards centre, with his hand to his eyes; MARY DOUL is seen on left coming forward softly.]

TIMMY [with blank amazement] Oh, the blind is wicked people, and it's no lie. But he'll walk off this day and not be troubling us more. [Turns back left and picks up MARTIN DOUL's coat and stick; some things fall out of coat pocket, which he gathers up again.]

MARTIN DOUL [turns round, sees MARY DOUL, whispers to MOLLY BYRNE with imploring agony] Let you not put shame on me, Molly, before herself and the smith. Let you not put shame on me, and I after saying fine words to you, and dreaming . . . dreams . . . in the night.[57] [He hesitates, and looks round the sky.] Is it a storm of thunder is coming, or the last end of the world? [He staggers towards MARY DOUL, tripping slightly over tin can.] The heavens is closing, I'm thinking, with darkness and great trouble passing in the sky. [He reaches MARY DOUL, and seizes her left arm with both his hands—with a frantic cry.] Is it the darkness of thunder is coming, Mary Doul? Do you see me clearly with your eyes?

MARY DOUL [snatches her arm away, and hits him with empty sack across the face] I see you a sight too clearly, and let you keep off from me now.[58]

MOLLY BYRNE [clapping her hands] That's right, Mary. That's the way to treat the like of him is after standing there at my feet and asking me to go off with him, till I'd grow an old wretched road woman the like of yourself.

MARY DOUL [defiantly] When the skin shrinks on your chin, Molly Byrne, there won't be the like of you for a shrunk hag in the four quarters of Ireland. . . . It's a fine pair you'd be, surely! [MARTIN DOUL is standing at back right centre, with his back to the audience.]

---

57. *and dreaming . . . dreams . . . in the night.* Possibly a Biblical echo—"and your young men shall see visions, and your old men dream dreams" *Acts* 2, 17.

58. *let you keep off from me now.* Prompt-book adds a stage direction: (*Martin staggers back RC and rests head on wall*).

TIMMY [*coming over to* MARY DOUL.] Is it no shame you have to let on she'd ever be the like of you?

MARY DOUL It's them that's fat and flabby do be wrinkled young, and that whitish yellowy hair she has does be soon turning the like of a handful of thin grass you'd see rotting, where the wet lies, at the north of a sty. [*Turning to go out on right.*] Ah, isn't it a grand thing for the like of you, maybe, to be setting fools mad a short while, and then to be turning a thing will drive off the little children[59] from your feet. [*She goes out.* MARTIN DOUL *has come forward again, mastering himself, but uncertain.*]

TIMMY Oh, God protect us, Molly, from the words of the blind. [*He throws down* MARTIN DOUL's *coat and stick.*] There's your old rubbish now, Martin Doul, and let you take it up, for it's all you have, and walk off through the world, and if ever[60] I meet you coming again, if it's seeing or blind you are itself, I'll bring out the big hammer and hit you a welt[61] with it will leave you easy[62] till the judgement day.

MARTIN DOUL [*rousing himself with an effort*] What call have you to talk the like of that with myself?

TIMMY [*pointing to* MOLLY BYRNE] It's well you know what call I have. It's well you know a decent girl, I'm thinking to wed, has no right to have her heart scalded with hearing talk—and queer, bad talk, I'm thinking—from a raggy-looking fool the like of you.

MARTIN DOUL [*raising his voice*] It's making game of you she is, for what seeing girl would marry with yourself? Look on him, Molly, look on him, I'm saying, for I'm seeing him still, and let you raise your voice, for the time is come, and bid him go up into his forge and be sitting there by himself, sneezing, and sweating, and he beating pot-hooks till the judgement day. [*He seizes her arm again.*]

MOLLY BYRNE Keep him off from me, Timmy!

---

59. *Ah, isn't it a grand thing . . . children* 1905: *Ah, it's a better thing to have a simple seemly face, the like of my face, for two score years, or fifty itself, than to be setting fools mad a short while, and then to be turning a thing would drive off the little children* The present text follows 1905 (JMS) rather than the slightly different prompt-book version. *Plays* I reads *the like of your make* in place of *the like of you, maybe*

60. *world, and if ever* 1905: *world, for if ever*

61. *welt* = blow.

62. *easy* = quiet.

TIMMY [pushing MARTIN DOUL aside] Would you have me strike you, Martin Doul? Go along now after your wife, who's a fit match for you, and leave Molly with myself.

MARTIN DOUL [despairingly] Won't you raise your voice, Molly, and lay hell's long curse on his tongue?

MOLLY BYRNE [on TIMMY's left] I'll be telling him it's destroyed I am with the sight of you and the sound of your voice. Go off now after your wife, and if she beats you again, let you go after the tinker girls is above running the hills, or down among the sluts of the town,[63] and you'll learn one day, maybe, the way a man should speak with a well-reared civil girl the like of me. [She takes TIMMY by the arm.] Come up now into the forge till he'll be gone down a bit on the road, for it's near afeard I am of the wild look he has come in his eyes. [She goes into the forge. TIMMY stops in the doorway.]

TIMMY Let me not find you out here again, Martin Doul. [He bares his arm.] It's well you know Timmy the smith has great strength in his arm, and it's a power of things it has broken a sight harder than the old bone of your skull. [He goes into the forge and pulls the door after him.]

MARTIN DOUL [stands a moment with his hand to his eyes] And that's the last thing I'm to set my sight on in the life of the world, the villainy of a woman and the bloody strength of a man. Oh, God, pity a poor blind fellow the way I am this day with no strength in me to do hurt to them at all. [He begins groping about for a moment, then stops.] Yet if I've no strength in me I've a voice left for my prayers, and may God blight them this day, and my own soul the same hour with them, the way I'll see them after, Molly Byrne and Timmy the smith, the two of them on a high bed, and they screeching in hell. . . . It'll be a grand thing that time to look on the two of them, and they twisting and roaring out, and twisting and roaring again, one day and the next day, and each day always and ever. It's not blind I'll be that time, and it won't be hell to me I'm thinking, but the like of Heaven itself, and it's fine care I'll be taking the Lord Almighty doesn't know.[64] [He turns to grope out.]

CURTAIN.

---

63. *and if she beats . . . town,* Cut in prompt-book.

64. *It'll be a grand . . . know.* Martin will endure damnation gladly for the pleasure of seeing Timmy and Molly in torment, but he will have to conceal his sadistic delight from God.

ACT III.

Scene: *Same as in first Act, but gap in centre has been filled with briars, or branches of some sort.* MARY DOUL, *blind again, gropes her way in on left, and sits as before. She has a few rushes with her. It is an early spring day.*

MARY DOUL *[mournfully]* Ah, God help me . . . God help me, the blackness wasn't so black at all the other time as it is this time, and it's destroyed I'll be now and hard set to get my living working alone, when it's few are passing and the winds are cold. *[She begins shredding rushes.]* I'm thinking short days will be long days to me from this time, and I sitting here, not seeing a blink, or hearing a word, and no thought in my mind but long prayers that Martin Doul'll get his reward in a short while for the villainy of his heart. It's great jokes the people'll be making now, I'm thinking, and they passing me by, pointing their fingers, maybe, and asking what place is himself, the way it's no quiet or decency I'll have from this day till I'm an old woman with long white hair and it twisting from my brow. *[She fumbles with her hair, and then seems to hear something. Listens for a moment.]* There's a queer slouching step coming on the road. . . . God help me, he's coming surely. *[She stays perfectly quiet. MARTIN DOUL gropes in on right, blind also.]*

MARTIN DOUL [gloomily]   The devil mend[65] Mary Doul
for putting lies on me, and letting on she was grand. The devil
mend the old saint for letting me see it was lies. [He sits down
near her.] The devil mend Timmy the smith for killing me
with hard work, and keeping me with an empty windy
stomach in me, in the day and in the night. Ten thousand
devils mend the soul of Molly Byrne [MARY DOUL nods her
head with approval] and the bad wicked souls is hidden in all the
women of the world. [He rocks himself, with his hand over his
face.] It's lonesome I'll be from this day, and if living people is
a bad lot, yet Mary Doul herself, and she a dirty, wrinkled-
looking hag,[66] was better maybe to be sitting along with than
no one at all. I'll be getting my death now, I'm thinking,
sitting alone in the cold air, hearing the night coming, and the
blackbirds flying round in the briars crying to themselves, the
time you'll hear one cart getting off a long way in the east, and
another cart getting off a long way in the west, and a dog
barking maybe, and a little wind turning the sticks. [He listens
and sighs heavily.] I'll be destroyed sitting alone and[67] losing
my senses this time the way I'm after losing my sight, for it'd
make any person afeard to be sitting up hearing the sound of
his breath [he moves his feet on the stones] and the noise of his
feet, when it's a power of queer things do be stirring, little
sticks breaking, and the grass moving [MARY DOUL half sighs,
and he turns on her in horror] till you'd take your dying oath on
sun and moon a thing was breathing on the stones. [He listens
towards her for a moment, then starts up nervously, and gropes about
for his stick.] I'll be going now, I'm thinking, but I'm not sure
what place my stick's in, and I'm destroyed with terror and
dread. [He touches her hand as he is groping about and cries out.]
There's a thing with a cold living hand[68] on it sitting up at my.
side. [He turns to run away, but misses his path and stumbles in
against the wall.] My road is lost on me now! Oh, merciful
God, set my foot on the path this day, and I'll be saying
prayers morning and night, and not straining my ear after
young girls, or doing any bad thing till I die—

---

65. *The devil mend*   The rationale of this curse is that the devil's cure is
worse than the affliction.

66. *and she a dirty, wrinkled-looking hag,*   Cut in the prompt-book.

67. *sitting alone and*   Cut in the prompt-book.

68. hand . . . *hand*   *1905:* face . . . *face*

MARY DOUL [indignantly] Let you not be telling lies to the Almighty God.

MARTIN DOUL Mary Doul is it? [Recovering himself with immense relief.] Is it Mary Doul, I'm saying?

MARY DOUL There's a sweet tone in your voice I've not heard for a space. You're taking me for Molly Byrne, I'm thinking.

MARTIN DOUL [coming towards her, wiping sweat from his face] Well, sight's a queer thing for upsetting a man. It's a queer thing to think I'd live to this day to be fearing the like of you, but if it's shaken I am for a short while, I'll soon be coming to myself.

MARY DOUL You'll be grand then, and it's no lie.

MARTIN DOUL [sitting down shyly, some way off] You've no call to be talking, for I've heard tell you're as blind as myself.

MARY DOUL If I am I'm bearing in mind I'm married to a little dark stump of a fellow looks the fool of the world, and I'll be bearing in mind from this day the great hullabuloo he's after making from hearing a poor woman breathing quiet in her place.

MARTIN DOUL And you'll be bearing in mind, I'm thinking, what you seen a while back when you looked down into a well, or a clear pool, maybe, when there was no wind stirring, and a good light in the sky.

MARY DOUL I'm minding that surely, for if I'm not the way the liars were saying below I seen a thing in them pools put joy and blessing in my heart. [She puts her hand to her hair again.]

MARTIN DOUL [laughing ironically] Well, they were saying below I was losing my senses but I never went any day the length of that. . . . God help you, Mary Doul, if you're not a wonder for looks, you're the maddest female woman is walking the counties of the east.

MARY DOUL [scornfully] You were saying all times you'd a great ear for hearing the lies in a word. A great ear, God help you, and you think you're using it now.

MARTIN DOUL If it's not lies you're telling, would you have me think you're not a wrinkled poor woman is looking like three scores, maybe, or two scores and a half?

MARY DOUL I would not, Martin. [She leans forward

earnestly.] For when I seen myself in them pools, I seen my hair would be gray or white maybe in a short while, and I seen with it that I'd a face would be a great wonder when it'll have soft white hair falling around it, the way when I'm an old woman there won't be the like of me surely in the seven counties of the east.

MARTIN DOUL *[with real admiration]* You're a cute[69] thinking woman, Mary Doul, and it's no lie.

MARY DOUL *[triumphantly]* I am surely, and I'm telling you a beautiful white-haired woman is a grand thing to see, for I'm told when Kitty Bawn[70] was selling poteen below, the young men itself would never tire to be looking in her face.

MARTIN DOUL *[taking off his hat and feeling his head, speaking with hesitation]* Did you think to look, Mary Doul, would there be a whiteness the like of that coming upon me?

MARY DOUL *[with extreme contempt]* On you, God help you? . . . In a short while you'll have a head on you as bald as an old turnip you'd see rolling round in the muck. You need never talk again of your fine looks, Martin Doul, for the day of that talk's gone for ever.

MARTIN DOUL That's a hard word to be saying, for I was thinking if I'd a bit of comfort, the like of yourself, it's not far off we'd be from the good days went before, and that'd be a wonder surely. But I'll never rest easy, thinking you're a gray, beautiful woman, and myself a pitiful show.

MARY DOUL I can't help your looks, Martin Doul. It wasn't myself made you with your rat's eyes, and your big ears, and your griseldy chin.

MARTIN DOUL *[rubs his chin ruefully, then beams with delight]* There's one thing you've forgot, if you're a cute thinking woman itself.

MARY DOUL Your slouching feet, is it? Or your hooky neck, or your two knees is black with knocking one on the other?

MARTIN DOUL *[with delighted scorn]* There's talking for a cute woman. There's talking surely!

MARY DOUL *[puzzled at the joy of his voice]* If you'd anything but lies to say you'd be talking yourself.

MARTIN DOUL *[bursting with excitement]* I've this to say,

---

69. *cute* See n. 11, p. 40.

70. *Kitty Bawn* = fair-haired Kitty—literally white Kitty.

Mary Doul. I'll be letting my beard grow in a short while, a beautiful, long, white, silken, streamy beard, you wouldn't see the like of in the eastern world.[71] . . . Ah, a white beard's a grand thing on an old man, a grand thing for making the quality stop and be stretching out their hands with good silver or gold, and a beard's a thing you'll never have so you may be holding your tongue.

MARY DOUL [laughing cheerfully] Well, we're a great pair, surely, and it's great times we'll have yet, maybe, and great talking before we die.

MARTIN DOUL Great times from this day with the help of the Almighty God, for a priest itself would believe the lies of an old man would have a fine white beard growing on his chin.

MARY DOUL There's the sound of one of them twittering yellow birds do be coming in the spring-time from beyond the sea, and there'll be a fine warmth now in the sun, and a sweetness in the air, the way it'll be a grand thing to be sitting here quiet and easy, smelling the things growing up, and budding from the earth.

MARTIN DOUL I'm smelling the furze a while back sprouting on the hill, and if you'd hold your tongue you'd hear the lambs of Grianan, though it's near drowned their crying is with the full river making noises in the glen.

MARY DOUL [listens] The lambs is bleating surely, and there's cocks and laying hens making a fine stir a mile off on the face of the hill. [She starts.]

MARTIN DOUL What's that is sounding in the west? [A faint sound of a bell is heard.]

MARY DOUL It's not the churches,[72] for the wind's blowing from the sea.

MARTIN DOUL [with dismay] It's the old saint, I'm thinking, ringing his bell.

MARY DOUL The Lord protect us from the saints of God! [They listen.] He's coming this road, surely.

---

71. the eastern world   Synge explained that "He does not mean here in the east of Ireland, but away in the 'eastern world,' a sort of wonderland very often spoken of in Irish folk-tales" (Plays I, p. 130).

72. it's not the churches,   Mary Doul here probably means Glendalough, often known in Wicklow as the Churches, short for the Seven Churches.

MARTIN DOUL *[tentatively]* Will we be running off, Mary Doul?

MARY DOUL What place would we run?

MARTIN DOUL There's the little path going up through the sloughs.[73] . . . If we reached the bank above, where the elders do be growing, no person would see a sight of us, if it was a hundred yeomen[74] were passing itself, but I'm afeard after the time we were with our sight we'll not find our way to it at all.

MARY DOUL *[standing up]* You'd find the way, surely. You're a grand man the world knows at finding your way if there was deep snow itself lying on the earth.[75]

MARTIN DOUL *[taking her hand]* Come a bit this way, it's here it begins. *[They grope about gap.]* There's a tree pulled into the gap, or a strange thing happened since I was passing it before.

MARY DOUL Would we have a right to be crawling in below under the sticks?

MARTIN DOUL It's hard set I am to know what would be right. And isn't it a poor thing to be blind when you can't run off itself, and you fearing to see?

MARY DOUL *[nearly in tears]* It's a poor thing, God help us, and what good'll our gray hairs be itself, if we have our sight, the way we'll see them falling each day, and turning dirty in the rain? *[The bell sounds near by.]*

MARTIN DOUL *[in despair]* He's coming now, and we won't get off from him at all.

MARY DOUL Could we hide in the bit of a briar[76] is growing at the west butt of the church?

MARTIN DOUL We'll try that, surely. *[He listens a moment.]* Let you make haste, I hear them trampling in the wood. *[They grope over to church.]*

MARY DOUL It's the words of the young girls making a great stir in the trees. *[They find the bush.]* Here's the briar on

---

73. *sloughs* = bogs.

74. *yeomen* The yeomanry were militia used by the English to quell the rebellion of 1798; they had left a folk memory as savage and relentless persecutors.

75. *your way . . . earth.* 1905: *your way winter or summer, if there was deep snow in it itself, or thick grass and leaves, maybe, growing from the earth.*

76. *in the bit of a briar* Prompt-book: *by the bit of a wall*

my left, Martin, I'll go in first, I'm the big one, and I'm easy to see.

MARTIN DOUL [*turning his head anxiously*]   It's easy heard you are, and will you be holding your tongue?

MARY DOUL [*partly behind bush*]   Come in now beside of me. [*They kneel down, still clearly visible.*] Do you think can they see us now, Martin Doul?

MARTIN DOUL   I'm thinking they can't, but I'm hard set to know, for the lot of them young girls, the devil save them, have sharp terrible eyes, would pick out a poor man I'm thinking, and he lying below hid in his grave.

MARY DOUL   Let you not be whispering sin, Martin Doul, or maybe it's the finger of God they'd see pointing to ourselves.

MARTIN DOUL   It's yourself is speaking madness, Mary Doul, haven't you heard the saint say it's the wicked do be blind?

MARY DOUL   If it is you'd have a right to speak a big terrible word would make the water not cure us at all.

MARTIN DOUL   What way would I find a big terrible word, and I shook with the fear, and if I did itself, who'd know rightly if it's good words or bad would save us this day from himself?

MARY DOUL   They're coming. I hear their feet on the stones. [SAINT *comes in on right with* TIMMY *and* MOLLY BYRNE *in holiday clothes, the others as before.*]

TIMMY   I've heard tell Martin Doul and Mary Doul were seen this day about on the road, holy father, and we were thinking you'd have pity on them and cure them again.

SAINT   I would, maybe, but where are they at all? I'll have little time left when I have the two of you wed in the church.

MAT SIMON [*at their seat*]   There are the rushes they do have lying round on the stones. It's not far off they'll be, surely.

MOLLY BYRNE [*pointing with astonishment*]   Look beyond, Timmy. [*They all look over and see* MARTIN DOUL.]

TIMMY   Well, Martin's a lazy fellow to be lying in there at the height of the day. [*He goes over shouting.*] Let you get up out of that. You were near losing a great chance by your sleepiness this day, Martin Doul. . . . The two of them's in it, God help us all!

MARTIN DOUL [*scrambling up with* MARY DOUL] What is it you want, Timmy, that you can't leave us in peace?

TIMMY The saint's come to marry the two of us, and I'm after speaking a word for yourselves, the way he'll be curing you now, for if you're a foolish man itself, I do be pitying you, for I've a kind heart, when I think[77] of you sitting dark again, and you after seeing a while, and working for your bread. [MARTIN DOUL *takes* MARY DOUL's *hand and tries to grope his way off right, he has lost his hat, and they are both covered with dust, and grass seeds.*]

PEOPLE You're going wrong. It's this way, Martin Doul. [*They push him over in front of* SAINT *near centre.* MARTIN DOUL *and* MARY DOUL *stand with piteous hang-dog dejection.*]

SAINT Let you not be afeard, for there's great pity with the Lord.

MARTIN DOUL We aren't afeard, holy father.

SAINT It's many a time those that are cured with the well of the four beauties of God lose their sight when a time is gone, but those I cure a second time, go on seeing till the hour of death. [*He takes the cover from his can.*] I've a few drops only left of the water, but, with the help of God, it'll be enough for the two of you, and let you kneel down now upon the road. [MARTIN DOUL *wheels round with* MARY DOUL *and tries to get away.*]

SAINT You can kneel down here, I'm saying, we'll not trouble this time going to the church.

TIMMY [*turning* MARTIN DOUL *round angrily*] Are you going mad in your head, Martin Doul? It's here you're to kneel. Did you not hear his reverence, and he speaking to you now?[78]

SAINT Kneel down, I'm saying, the ground's dry at your feet.

MARTIN DOUL [*with distress*] Let you go on your own way, holy father. We're not calling you at all.

SAINT I'm not saying a word of penance, or fasting itself, so you've no call[79] now to be fearing me, but let you

---

77. *yourselves . . . think* Prompt-book: *yourselves, for I do be pitying you, when I think*

78. *It's here . . . now?* Prompt-book: *Did you not hear his reverence say it's here you're to kneel?*

79. *fasting itself, so you've no call* 1905: *fasting itself, for I'm thinking the Lord has brought you great teaching in the blinding of your eyes, so you've no call*

kneel down till I give you your sight.

MARTIN DOUL [more troubled] We're not asking our sight, holy father, and let you be walking on and leaving us in our peace[80] at the crossing roads, for it's best we are this way, and we're not asking to see.

SAINT [to PEOPLE] Is his mind gone that he's no wish to be cured this day, and looking out on the wonders of the world?

MARTIN DOUL It's wonders enough I seen in a short space, holy father, for the life of one man only.

TIMMY Is it he see wonders?

PATCH He's making game.

MAT SIMON He's maybe drunk, holy father.[81]

SAINT [puzzled] I never heard tell of any person wouldn't have great joy to be looking on the earth, and the image of the Lord thrown upon men.

MARTIN DOUL [raising his voice, by degrees] That's great sights holy father. . . . What was it I seen my first day, but your own bleeding feet and they cut with the stones, and my last day, but the villainy of herself you're wedding, God forgive you, to Timmy the smith. . . . That was great sights maybe. . . . And wasn't it great sights seeing the roads when the north winds would be driving and the skies would be harsh, and you'd see the horses and the asses and the dogs itself, maybe, with their heads hanging and they closing their eyes.

TIMMY There's talking.

MAT SIMON He's maybe right, it's lonesome living when the days are dark.

MOLLY BYRNE He's not right. Let you speak up holy father, and confound him now.[82]

SAINT [coming close to MARTIN DOUL and putting his hand on his shoulder][83] Did you never hear tell of the summer and the fine spring in places where the holy men of Ireland have built up churches to the Lord, that you'd wish to be closed

---

80. *let you be walking . . . peace* 1905: *let you walk on your own way, and be fasting, or praying, or doing anything that you will, but leave us here in our peace*

81. TIMMY *Is it he . . . holy father.* Not in *1905*.

82. TIMMY *There's . . . him now.* Not in *1905*.

83. [coming . . . shoulder]. Not in *1905*.

up[84] and seeing no sight of the glittering seas, and the furze is opening above, will soon have the hills shining as if it was fine creels[85] of gold they were, rising to the sky?

PATCH   That's it, holy father.

MAT SIMON   What will you say now, Martin Doul?[86]

MARTIN DOUL [fiercely]   I'll say it's ourselves have finer sight than the lot of you, and we sitting abroad in the sweetness of the warmth of night [SAINT draws back from him] hearing a late thrush, maybe, and the swift flying things[87] do be racing in the air, till we do be looking up in our own minds into a grand sky, and seeing lakes and broadening rivers and hills are waiting for the spade and plough.

MAT SIMON [roaring laughing]   It's songs he's making now, holy father.

PATCH   It's mad he is.[88]

MOLLY BYRNE   It's not but lazy, holy father, and not wishing to work, for a while since he was all times longing and screeching for the light of day.

MARTIN DOUL [with vehement bitterness]   If I was, I seen my fill in a short while with the look of my wife, and the look of your own wicked grin Molly Byrne, the time you're making game with a man.

MOLLY BYRNE   There's talking. . . . Let you not mind him more, holy father, but leave him in darkness if it's that is best fitting the blackness of his heart.[89]

---

84. *Lord, that you'd wish to be closed up*   1905: *Lord? No man isn't a madman, I'm thinking, would be talking the like of that, and wishing to be closed up*

85. *creels* = "tall baskets or hampers for fish or turf'—Synge's note (*Plays* I, p. 140).

86. PATCH   *That's it . . . Martin Doul?*   Not in *1905*.

87. MARTIN DOUL [fiercely . . . *flying things*   1905: Martin Doul. *Is it talking now you are of Knock and Ballavore? Ah, it's ourselves had finer sights than the like of them, I'm telling you, when we were sitting a while back hearing the birds and bees humming in every weed of the ditch, or when we'd be smelling the sweet beautiful smells does be rising in the warm nights, when you do hear the swift flying things*

88. MAT SIMON [roaring . . . *he is.*   1905: Saint. [To People.] *There's little use talking with the like of him.*

89. *There's talking . . . heart.*   1905: *Let you not mind, holy father, for it's bad things he was saying to me awhile back—bad things for a married man, your reverence—and you'd do right surely to leave him in Darkness, if it's that is best fitting the villainy of his heart.*

TIMMY   Cure Mary Doul, your reverence, who is a quiet poor woman never said a hard word but when she'd be vexed with himself, or with the young girls do be making game of her below.

MAT SIMON   That's it. Cure Mary Doul, your reverence.[90]

SAINT   There's little use I'm thinking, talking to the like of him, but if you've any sense[91] Mary Doul, let you kneel down at my feet, and I'll bring sight into your eyes.

MARTIN DOUL*[more defiantly]*   You will not, holy father. . . . Would you have her looking on me and saying hard words to me till the hour of death?

SAINT *[severely]*   If she's wanting her sight I wouldn't have the like of you stop her at all. *[To MARY DOUL.]* Kneel down, I'm saying.

MARY DOUL *[confused]*   Let us be as we are, holy father, and then we'll be known again in a short while as the people is happy and blind, and we'll be having an easy time, with no trouble to live, and we getting halfpence on the road.

MOLLY BYRNE   Let you not be raving. Kneel down and get your sight, and let himself be taking halfpence if he likes it best.

TIMMY   If it's choosing a wilful blindness you are, there isn't anyone will give you a hap'worth[92] of meal, or be doing the little things you do need to keep you living in the world at all.

MAT SIMON   If you had your sight you could be keeping a watch on him that no other woman came near in the night or day.[93]

MARY DOUL *[partly convinced]*   That's true maybe.[94]

SAINT   Kneel down, for I must be hastening with the marriage, and going my own way before the fall of night.

---

90. MAT SIMON   *That's . . . reverence.*   Not in *1905.*

91. SAINT   *There's . . . sense*   *1905:* Saint [to Mary Doul.] *If you have any sense*

92. *hap'worth*   Short for "halfpennyworth," pronounced hayperth.

93. *sight . . . day.*   *1905: sight, Mary, you could be walking up for him and down with him, and be stitching his clothes, and keeping a watch on him day and night the way no other woman would come near him at all.*

94. MARY DOUL [partly convinced] *That's true maybe.*   *1905:* Mary Doul. [Half persuaded]. *That's the truth, maybe—*

PEOPLE *[together]* Kneel down, Mary! Kneel down when you're bid by the saint!

MARY DOUL *[looking uneasily towards* MARTIN DOUL*]* Maybe it's right they are, and I will if you wish it, holy father. *[She kneels down.* SAINT *takes off his hat and gives it to some one near him. All the men take off their hats.]*

SAINT *[goes forward a step to take* MARTIN DOUL's *hand away from* MARY DOUL*]* Go aside now, we're not wanting you here.

MARTIN DOUL *[pushes him away roughly, and stands with his left hand on* MARY DOUL's *shoulder]* Keep off yourself, holy father, and let you not be taking my rest from me in the darkness of my wife. . . . What call had the like of you coming where you're not wanted, and making[95] a great mess, with the holy water you have and the length of your prayers? *[Defiantly.]* Go on, I'm saying, and leave us this place on the road.

SAINT If it was a seeing man I heard talking the like of that I'd put a black curse on him would weigh down his soul till it'd be falling to hell, but you're a poor blind sinner, God forgive you, and I don't mind you at all. *[He raises his can.]* Go aside now, till I give the blessing to your wife, and if you won't go of your own will, there are those standing by will make you, surely.

MARTIN DOUL Well, there's bitter hardness in the pity of your like, and what is it you want coming for to break our happiness and hour of ease. Let you rise up, Mary, and not heed them more. *[Pulls* MARY DOUL.*]*[96]

SAINT *[imperiously, to* PEOPLE*]* Let you take that man and drive him down upon the road.

MAT SIMON Come on now.

PATCH Come on from talking badness to the holy saint. *[They seize* MARTIN DOUL.*]*

MARTIN DOUL *[throwing himself down on the ground]* I'll not come I'm saying, and let you take his holy water to cure the blackness of your souls today.

MARY DOUL Leave him easy, holy father, when I'd liefer live dark all times beside him, than be getting eyesight

---

95. *What call . . . making 1905: What call has the like of you to be coming between married people—that you're not understanding at all—and be making*

96. MARTIN DOUL *Well . . .* DOUL] *1905:* Martin Doul. [Pulling Mary Doul.] *Come along now, and don't mind him at all.*

for new torments now.

SAINT   You have taken your choice. Drag him off from her I'm saying.

PEOPLE   That's it. That's it. Come forward till we drop him in the pool beyond.[97]

MARTIN DOUL [screaming]   Make them leave me go holy father. Make them leave me go I'm saying, and let you not think badly of my heathen talk,[98] but cure her this day and do anything you will.

SAINT [to PEOPLE]   Let him be. Let him be, if his sense has come to him at all. [MARTIN DOUL rises and pulls himself together, stands beside MARY DOUL.]

MARTIN DOUL [sinking his voice to a plausible whine]   You will do well to cure her holy father, I wouldn't stop you at all . . . it's great joy she'll have looking on your face . . . but let you cure me along with her, the way I'll see when it's lies she's telling, and be looking out day and night upon the holy men of God. [He kneels down a little before MARY DOUL.]

SAINT [with great piety][99]   Men who are dark a long while, and thinking queer thoughts in their heads, aren't the like of simple men, who do be working every day, and praying, and living like ourselves, so if he's found a right mind at the last minute itself, I'll take pity on him, and cure him, if the Lord will, and not be thinking on the hard foolish words he's after saying this day to us all.

MARTIN DOUL [listening eagerly]   I'm waiting holy father.

SAINT [with can in his hand, close to MARTIN DOUL]   With the power of the water from the grave of the four beauties of God— [He raises can.][100] [MARTIN DOUL with a sudden movement strikes the can from SAINT's hand and sends it rocketing across stage.]

PEOPLE [with a terrified murmur]   Will you look what he's done? Oh, glory be to God.[101]

---

97. MAT SIMON   Come on now . . . pool beyond.   Not in 1905.

98. and let you not think badly of my heathen talk,   Not in 1905.

99. SAINT [with great piety].   1905: Saint. [Speaking half to the People].

100. God—[He raises can.]   1905: God, with the power of this water I'm saying that I put upon your eyes—[He raises can.]

101. PEOPLE [with a terrified . . . . God.   1905: [People murmur loudly.]

MARTIN DOUL *[stands up triumphantly and pulls* MARY DOUL *up]* If I'm a poor dark sinner I've sharp ears, God help me, and it's well I heard the little splash of the water you had there in the can. Go on now, holy father, for if you're a fine saint itself, it's more sense is in a blind man, and more power maybe than you're thinking at all. Let you walk on now with your worn feet, and your welted knees and your fasting holy ways have left you with a big head on you and a thin pitiful arm.

PEOPLE   Go on from this.[102] *[*SAINT *looks at him for a moment severely, then turns away and picks up his can.]*

MARTIN DOUL   We're going surely,[103] for if it's a right some of you have to be working and sweating the like of Timmy the smith, and a right some of you have to be fasting and praying and talking holy talk the like of yourself, I'm thinking it's a good right ourselves have to be sitting blind, hearing a soft wind turning round the little leaves of the spring and feeling the sun, and we not tormenting our souls with the sight of the gray days, and the holy men, and the dirty feet is trampling the world. *[He gropes towards his stone with* MARY DOUL.*]*

MAT SIMON   It'd be an unlucky fearful thing, I'm thinking to have the like of that man living near us at all.[104] Wouldn't he bring down a curse upon us, holy father, from the heavens of God?

SAINT *[tying his girdle]*   God has great mercy, but great wrath for them that sin.

PEOPLE[105]   Go on now, Martin Doul. Go on from this place. Let you not be bringing great storms or droughts on us

---

102. PEOPLE   *Go on from this.*   Not in *1905;* added in TCD MSS.

103. MARTIN DOUL   *We're going surely,*   Not in *1905;* added in TCD MSS.

104. *living near us at all.*   *1905: living near us at all in the townland of Grianan,*

105. Prompt-book shows the distribution of the People's lines:

		The People
2b	*Girls*	Go on now, Martin Doul
	Men	Go on from this place

1a	*Timmy*	Let you not be bringing great storms
	Mat Simon	or droughts on us

The final phrase *maybe, from the power of the Lord* was cut.

maybe from the power of the Lord. *[Some of them throw things at him.]*

MARTIN DOUL *[turning round defiantly]*[106] Keep off now the yelping lot of you, or it's more than one maybe will get a bloody head on him from the welt of my stick.[107] Keep off now, and let you not be afeard, for we're going on the two of us to the towns of the south, where the people will have kind voices maybe, and we won't know their bad looks or their villainy at all.[108]

MARY DOUL *[despondingly]* That's the truth, surely, and we'd have a right to be gone, if it's a long way itself, where[109] you do have to be walking with a slough of wet on the one side and a slough of wet on the other, and you going a stony path with a north wind blowing behind.

PEOPLE Go on now. Go on from this place.

MARTIN DOUL Keep off I'm saying. *[He takes MARY DOUL's hand.]* Come on now and we'll be walking to the south, for we've seen too much of everyone in this place, and it's small joy we'd have living near them, or hearing the lies they do be telling from the gray of dawn till the night. *[They go.]*

TIMMY There's a power of deep rivers with floods in them where you do have to be lepping the stones and you going to the south, so I'm thinking the two of them will be drowned together in a short while, surely.

SAINT They have chosen their lot, and the Lord have mercy on their souls. *[He rings his bell.]* And let the two of you come up now into the church, Molly Byrne and Timmy the smith, till I make your marriage and put my blessing on you all. *[He turns to the church, procession forms, and the curtain comes down, as they go slowly into the church.]*

CURTAIN.

---

106. MARTIN DOUL [turning round defiantly] *1905:* Martin Doul. [Turning round defiantly and picking up a stone.]

107. *from the welt of my stick. 1905: from the pitch of my stone*

108. In *1905* Martin Doul's two last speeches were one, followed by Mary Doul's *That's the truth . . . blowing behind.*

109. *itself, where 1905: itself, as I've heard them say, where*